Essays in International Trade and Public Economics

FINANZWISSENSCHAFTLICHE SCHRIFTEN

Herausgegeben von den Professoren
Konrad, Krause-Junk, Littmann †, Oberhauser, Pohmer

Band 122

PETER LANG
Frankfurt am Main · Berlin · Bern · Bruxelles · New York · Oxford · Wien

Margarita M. Kalamova

Essays in International Trade and Public Economics

PETER LANG
Internationaler Verlag der Wissenschaften

Bibliographic Information published by the Deutsche Nationalbibliothek
The Deutsche Nationalbibliothek lists this publication in the Deutsche Nationalbibliografie; detailed bibliographic data is available in the internet at http://dnb.d-nb.de.

Zugl.: Berlin, Freie Univ., Diss., 2009

Cover Design:
Atelier Platen, Friedberg

D 188
ISSN 0170-8252
ISBN 978-3-631-62139-4

www.peterlang.de

To my parents

Contents

Acknowledgements

I would like to thank my supervisor, Kai A. Konrad, for his guidance and support through these years. I would also like to thank my second advisor, Sebastian G. Kessing, for his continuous feedback and opportune advice.

I am grateful for having had the opportunity to work on my dissertation project in the motivating and stimulating environment of the Social Science Research Center Berlin (WZB). Special thanks are due to my colleagues from the research unit Market Processes and Governance: Aron Kiss, Salmai Qari, Benny Geys, Florian Morath, Beate Jochimsen, Johannes Münster, Robert Nuscheler, Marie-Laure Breuille and Nelly Exbrayat, who always encouraged me and supported my work with insightful comments. Furthermore, I would like to thank Nina Bonge for the valuable technical support and Babette Hagemann for welcoming me at WZB and helping me overcome many bureaucratic hurdles.

I appreciate the financial support from the WZB and the German Science Foundation's (DFG) Priority Programme on Federalism which allowed me to visit meetings of a network of distinguished researchers as well as to present my research at international conferences and workshops in Austria, Bulgaria, Canada, Germany, Greece, Hungary, Italy, Switzerland, Turkey and the USA.

I would like to express my gratitude for insightful conversations and helpful suggestions from colleagues from the Berlin universities and research institutes, in particular, Runli Xie, Fang Yao, Atanas Hristov, Julianne Scheffel, Tomaso Duso, Ela Glowicka, Michal Grajek, Jo Seldeslachts and Monika Kerekes.

I would like to thank all the marvelous people who made my life warmer and the process of writing this thesis more productive during the years. I can't help thanking Adim for the patience and willingness to help; Aron for the support and practical advice; Samera, Runli and Atanas for revising my English and German and cheering me up; and Imola, Sophia Bickhardt and Mrs. Katzarova for the stimulating conversations at any time. I also thank my brilliant sister for her technical support, in particular, during the last weeks before the finalization of this thesis. I am indefinitely indebted to them all.

Finally and most importantly, I deeply thank my parents for their unconditional support and unshaken belief in me; they made this whole journey possible. And my husband for our flourishing relationship.

Chapter 1

Introduction

The present thesis is a collection of three essays in International Trade and Public Economics. They all deal with the relationship between the structure and quality of the public sector and the process of economic integration. Furthermore, all three of them use the tools and methods of panel data econometrics in their investigation analyses. Chapters 2 and 3 study the impact of government architecture, in particular, the degree and form of government decentralization on trade and foreign direct investment, respectively. Chapter 4 considers additionally the effect of governments' intangible assets on foreign direct investment.

The introductory chapter is organized as follows: The next section is dedicated to the main results and theories in the international trade literature. Section 1.2 presents important insights about the architecture of government won from the public finance literature. Section 1.3 summarizes the main contributions of the three essays in relation to the literature in international trade and public economics.

1.1 The study of international trade

The study of international trade is preoccupied with the question under what conditions firms decide to serve foreign markets through exports and (or) establishing an affiliate abroad. This section gives an overview of the theoretical insights and empirical results from the literature on trade and foreign direct investment. In particular, the role of the gravity equation in trade research and of similar general-equilibrium models in the research on multinational enterprises will be emphasized.

1.1.1 On the gravity model in trade

According to Newton's "Law of Universal Gravitation" two bodies are attracted to each other in proportion to the product of their mass and in inverse proportion to the square of the distance separating them. In 1962 Jan Tinbergen proposed in his seminal work "Shaping the World Economy" that roughly the same functional form could be applied to international trade flows. The gravity model, as the modified gravitation theory is known in social science, takes into account the economic size of two regions and the distance between them. Because larger regions attract goods more than smaller ones and the closer regions interact more with each other, the gravity model incorporates these two features. In the traditional version of the gravity model, bilateral trade flows are positively correlated with the size of each partner and negatively affected by the level of trade costs, including distance. The multiplicative form of the gravity equation allows for a simple log-linear estimation, which has made it the "workhorse for empirical studies" in international economics (Eichengreen and Irwin 1998). It has proved to be the most robust empirical relationship explaining bilateral flows of goods, people and capital.

Empirical implementations. The large empirical literature on trade using the gravity equation provides a number of basic facts: i) trade diminishes dramatically with distance and trade costs; ii) trade costs are large; iii) national borders diminish trade volumes; and iv) trade liberalizing agreements have mixed effect on trade.

Trade costs are large (an overview of the literature is provided by Anderson and van Wincoop 2004). Trade costs are defined as all costs incurred in getting a good to a final user other than the marginal production cost of the good itself. Generally, they can be classified into four types. First, natural barriers result from geography like distance, access to sea, common border, or common language. On average, a 10 percent increase in distance lowers bilateral trade by about 9 percent and the effect is found to be persistent over time and across different samples and methodologies[1]. Hummels (2001), for instance, can show that non-speaking a common language increases costs by 7 percent. The second type of trade barriers, transport costs, as measured by freight charges and insurance but also indirect transport user costs (for example, time delay, inventory costs, preparation costs) have slightly declined, on average, in the last decades with air freight cost falling dramatically, but ocean shipping cost rising (Hummels 1999).

Third, the literature differentiates between tariff and non-tariff policy barriers to trade. Evidence suggests that variation of tariffs across goods is quite large in all countries, which adds to the welfare loss of tariffs themselves (Anderson and Neary 2003). On the bilateral level Harrigan (1993) reports very low production-weighted average tariffs in 28 product categories for OECD countries. In comparison to tariffs, non-tariff barriers are much more difficult to quantify and although they are concentrated in a smaller number of sectors, their tax equivalents seem to be very high (Deardorff and Stern 1998). Messerlin (2001) combines tariff and non-tariff barriers and reports strikingly high tax equivalents for some industries, such as 100.3 percent for dairy products, 125 percent for sugar, and 71.3 percent in mining. In the context of tariffs it is important to mention the large body of literature testing the relationship between free trade agreements and international trade. The results have been mixed in the past with several studies indicating some positive effect of free

[1] Disdier and Head (2008) arrive at the result by constructing a database of 1,467 estimates from 103 papers and estimating the mean effect of distance to be about 0.9.

trade agreements on trade (Tinbergen 1962, Aitken 1973), others insignificant effect (Bergstrand 1985, Rose 2004), and some even negative effect (Frankel et al. 1997). However, recent works which address the potential endogeneity bias in estimating the effect of trade policies on trade volumes (Baier and Bergstrand 2007) and base their analysis on the gravity equation of Anderson and van Wincoop (2003)[2] stress the robust and strongly positive role of free trade agreements on trade flows.

Forth, a novel addition to the set of trade cost variables is the famous *border effect* proposed by McCallum (1995)[3]. He compares intra-national trade between Canadian provinces to international trade between Canadian provinces and US states using 1998 data, just before the Canada-US free trade agreement was signed, and shows that two Canadian provinces trade 22 times more with each other than with US states of similar size and distance. A large amount of subsequent research has illustrated that domestic trade volumes usually tend to be two to twenty times larger than international trade volumes. By using country-level instead of regional trade data Wei (1996) and Nitsch (2000) find out that an average OECD and EU country imports about two and half and seven to ten times more to itself than to an otherwise identical partner country, respectively, after adjustment for sizes, distance, common language, common border and remoteness. Wolf (2000) indicates a home bias for traded goods within versus across US states of a magnitude at three. The magnitude of the border effect seems to depend on the measure of internal distance as argued in Helliwell and Verdier (2001). They find higher estimates of internal distances, and hence border effects, than found in previous studies. Chen (2004) confirms that the way distance is measured matters dramatically for the size of the border effect. Moreover, the author shows that technical barriers to trade tend to increase border effects. An additional insight is that agglomeration of intermediate and final goods producers also reduces the need for cross-border trade and thus increases the home bias (as in Chen 2004 and Wolf 2000, for instance).

[2]Their model has become the working horse in the empirical trade literature and will be discussed in more detail below.

[3]The border effect is a dummy variable which is equal to 1 for intra-national trade flows and 0 otherwise (for international trade).

While it is not surprising that national borders create a barrier to the free flow of goods, it is the size of the effect that is puzzling. Anderson and van Wincoop (2003) show that the border effect is equal to the product of two factors: the degree of substitutability between goods produced in different countries and the tariff equivalent of the border barrier[4]. Furthermore, they argue that most studies (including some of those discussed above) suffer from omitted variables bias which tends to overestimate the border effect. In equilibrium bilateral trade depends on both exporter and importer price levels, which are themselves functions of trade barriers, the so-called multilateral resistance terms. However, until the emergence of their seminal work no empirical study has accounted for the existence of relative price terms in the gravity equation. Anderson and van Wincoop (2003) use a sophisticated computational non-linear method, which estimates the multilateral resistance terms with respect to all trading pairs simultaneously. However, although their method provides consistent and efficient estimates of the border effect, its major drawback is that it requires custom programming. Feenstra (2002) recommends the use of exporter and importer country fixed effects to measure the price indexes, since the two methods produce identical results and the latter is simple to implement. In contrast, as stressed by Feenstra (2002), the use of published data on price indexes (as in Bergstrand 1985, 1989) cannot accurately account for multilateral resistance, since the border is not reflected in aggregate price indexes. In an alternative approach Baier and Bergstrand (2007, 2009) decompose the influences of multilateral resistance and nonlinearity which enables them to use linear estimator.

Theoretical foundations. Although the gravity model provides a good fit to most data sets of regional and international trade flows, the absence of strong theoretical foundations in the past inhibited its use for policy. The theory to the gravity equation was initiated by Anderson (1979) who is the first to explain its multiplicative form. For the purpose he uses an Armington-like product differentiation setting with perfect competition. His model builds on the properties of expenditure systems and makes inferences about regions with similar traded-

[4]Chen (2004) has already been mentioned in this context. See also Wei (1996) and Evans (2003).

goods preferences and trade cost structures. In particular, the theory tells us that after controlling for size, trade between two regions is decreasing in their bilateral trade barrier relative to the average barrier of the two regions to trade with all their partners. Through Anderson and van Wincoop's (2003) influential work "Gravity with Gravitas: A Solution to the Border Puzzle" this theory has become the most widely recognized possible foundation of the gravity equation. Anderson and van Wincoop (2003) build on the constant-elasticity-of-substitution expenditure framework of Anderson (1979) and differentiate goods by country of origin to derive an operational gravity model, which includes both bilateral and multilateral trade barriers[5].

Regarding monopolistic competition as an alternative microeconomic foundation for the gravity equation, Bergstrand (1985) is the first to use a general-equilibrium model including monopolistic competition. The main outcome of his study is the emergence of price terms as important determinants of trade flows, which lends behavioral content to the gravity equation. Bergstrand (1989) extends his previous work by offering an analytical framework for understanding the gravity equation that is consistent with theories of inter-industry and intra-industry trade. He provides an explicit theoretical foundation for exporter and importer incomes and per capita incomes by incorporating relative factor-endowment differences in the spirit of Heckscher-Ohlin. Deardorff (1998) also derives the gravity equation from a model in which countries are fully specialized in differentiated goods.

In the studies described above complete specialization of production and identical preferences generate the force of gravity. The search for further theoretical explanations of the gravity equation has produced works that distinguish the sources of specialization (Feenstra et al. 2001) and investigate whether incomplete specialization can derive the gravity equation (Evenett and Keller 2002). Feenstra et al. (2001) discriminate among theories of specialization by examining differences between the elasticities of bilateral trade with respect to importer and exporter income. They show that in a model with free entry and

[5]Their theory has significant applications to the border effect between the United States and Canada discussed in the empirical section.

monopolistic competition own-income elasticity of exports is larger than the importer-income elasticity, but the reverse result holds in models with restricted entry, including Armington national differentiation models and oligopolistic reciprocal dumping models. In a world of two countries the Ricardian model of Evenett and Keller (2002) makes clear predictions about bilateral trade. Their model leads to a gravity equation for an aggregate of homogenous goods. By extending the analysis to a world of more than two countries, Haveman and Hummels (2004) also derive the gravity equation from a model of incomplete specialization. More importantly, by accounting for homogenous goods, differences in preferences, and fixed costs, the authors can generalize the theoretical model predictions developed by Anderson and van Wincoop (2003). A further generalization of Anderson and van Wincoop's (2003) gravity equation has been recently made by Helpman et al. (2008) by using a model of international trade in differentiated products in which firms face fixed and variable costs of exporting. As a result, they can predict an extensive margin for trade flows and account for asymmetric trade flows between the trading partners.

1.1.2 On the general-equilibrium approach in FDI

Ideally, the literature on foreign direct investment (FDI) would have an established model and empirical specification as the gravity equation in the trade literature. As with trade flows, a gravity specification fits cross-country data on FDI reasonably well. However, there is no similar paper to Anderson and van Wincoop (2003) that lays out a tractable model which specifically identifies gravity variables as the sole determinants of FDI patterns. In fact, intuition and theory suggests that the behavior of multinational enterprises (MNEs) and FDI is likely to be much more complicated to model than trade flows. After first presenting the main theoretical insights of the MNE literature, in the empirical session I will discuss the most common empirical frameworks and their applications.

Theoretical insights. In the recent three decades, multinational flows have grown at high rates, outpacing the remarkable expansion of goods trade. This increased importance of MNEs has motivated the theoretical research to produce a number of general equilibrium models for the analysis of MNEs' decisions. Since Helpman (1984) and Markusen (1984), general equilibrium theory has suggested two very distinct motivations for FDI: to access low factor prices for the production process (vertical FDI) and access markets in the face of trade frictions (horizontal FDI).

Helpman (1984) and Helpman and Krugman (1985) emphasize the difference in relative factor endowments between the source and host country as the factor which brings about the emergence of vertical MNEs. The theory refers to single-plant firms which maximize profits and make cost-minimizing location choices of product lines. It predicts that a corporation will become a multinational if the source country is (human) capital-intensive, while the host country is labor-abundant, which automatically supposes one-directional vertical MNE activity from the developed countries, richly endowed with capital, to the less-developed ones, richly endowed with labor. Another important implication of the theory is that it explains the simultaneous existence of intersectoral trade, intra-industry trade, and intra-firm trade.

The horizontal model of MNE activity, which traces back to Markusen (1984), assumes multi-plant companies which produce the same good in various countries for serving the local markets. Confronted by trade and distance costs, firms in this theory achieve the best possible market access by establishing an affiliate abroad rather than by exporting. Compared to the factor-proportion model of Helpman (1984) this theory can explain two-way international activities, and, in particular, activities between similarly developed countries[6].

Recently, Markusen (2002) and Markusen and Venables (1998, 2000) have combined these two models into the so-called knowledge-capital (KC) framework. The model is characterized by two countries, two factors, a perfectly competitive homogenous goods sector and a second sector, which is a Cournot oligopoly. In this KC model, firms decide whether to vertically differentiate, to horizontally fragment production or to serve the foreign market through ex-

[6]Other theoretical models on horizontal FDI include Horstmann and Markusen (1987, 1992).

ports. The theory predicts that horizontal MNE dominate when countries have similar relative endowments and sizes. Furthermore, horizontal FDI is encouraged by higher trade costs and higher firm-level scale economies. In contrast, vertical FDI is greatest when countries have very different endowments. The combination of small size and skilled-labor abundance leads to vertical firms, which choose the skilled-labor abundant country as their headquarters country, while the location of a single-plant depends on market size.

Other recent models depart from the firm-symmetry assumption of the theories described above and consider the importance of firm heterogeneity for internalization decisions. Melitz (2003) and Helpman et al. (2004, 2008) highlight the important role of within-sector firm productivity differences in explaining the decision of a firm to become multinational. Their model clearly predicts that only the most productive firms engage in foreign activities, and among these firms, only the most productive will locate a subsidiary abroad because the latter can pay the fixed costs associated with setting up a business abroad. Low-productivity firms choose to serve only the domestic market and the least productive ones leave the industry. And although this literature makes important contribution to the theory of horizontal MNEs, it is not able to distinguish between different patterns of production fragmentation.

Empirical implementations. Translating MNE general-equilibrium theory to an empirical specification is a challenging issue which emerges mainly from the complexity of the underlying theoretical models. Since the models, in general, cannot provide closed-form solutions, predictions are made rather on the basis of simulations. In this section I concentrate mainly on the empirics of the KC model[7]. This model has received wide recognition in applied FDI research, since it provides the theoretical basis for empirically assessing the importance of the horizontal and the vertical model against the general KC model. Furthermore, Chapters 3 and 4 of this thesis use extended versions of the KC model in their empirical analysis.

[7]For an elaborate overview of the empirical literature on FDI I refer to Blonigen (2005).

Carr et al. (2001) demonstrate the first empirical specification of the KC model[8]. It results from numerical simulations of the model and describes affiliate sales in a host country as a function of GDP of the source and host countries, trade costs of the two countries, investment costs of the host, and differences in factor endowments between the source and the host, the so-called "skill differences". The sum and difference of gross domestic products (GDPs) together with interactions between them and "skill difference" account for the non-linear structure of the simulated results. Inferences about the investment modes – horizontal or vertical – are based on the signs of the last variables. Positive coefficients for GDP sum and the host trade costs, and a negative one for GDP difference is in line with horizontal FDI, while a negative sign for skill difference implies vertical fragmentation of production. Using a panel dataset of US outward and inward affiliate sales for the period 1986-1994, the authors find consistent evidence for the horizontal and vertical mode of FDI.

In a response to Blonigen et al. (2003) critique about the skill difference variable being always negative for US inbound affiliate sales, a subsequent study by Markusen and Maskus (2002) clarifies and improves the original specification. To the existing interaction term between GDP difference and skill difference they add two other interactions - between GDP sum and skill difference. The first term takes non-zero values when the parent country is skilled-labor abundant and it is larger the larger the degree of relative factor endowment and total two-country income. It is predicted by the vertical investment model to have a positive sign. The second interaction is non-zero when the host country is skilled-labor abundant and is larger the larger the relative endowment difference. It is predicted to have a negative sign as by all three models (horizontal, vertical, and KC). By using the same dataset as in Carr et al. (2001, 2003) they receive strong support for the KC model, but cannot distinguish it from the horizontal model. However, their main message is that the vertical model cannot fit to the real data on FDI activity.

[8]Brainard (1997) is the first to match predictions of a general-equilibrium model of MNE to data. She derives an equation for the proportion of MNE sales that are exports to total foreign sales. Her model is not considered in detail in this work, since it departs from the theoretical frameworks described above.

The last result has motivated the emergence of several studies which try to resolve the puzzle of missing evidence on vertical production fragmentation. By re-defining the KC model as described in Carr et al. (2001), Braconier et al. (2005) find firm and robust evidence in favor of the KC model and its vertical component. They replace GDP difference between the source and host country with a variable measuring the size of the source country and suggest another definition of the skill variable. The two new variables are geometrically derived from the Edgeworth box, which proves to be crucial for their results. The authors indicate two main reasons for the "missing" vertical FDI: the limited dataset of previous studies and the use of skill measure which becomes increasingly biased as the source country's skill-intensity increases. Davies (2008) also "hunts high and low" for vertical FDI by changing slightly the original specification of Carr et al. (2001). He improves the model by accounting for non-monotonicities in skill differences when the parent is skill-labor abundant. As a result he can reject the horizontal model in favor of the more comprehensive KC model when measuring FDI activity by the stock of FDI. Nevertheless, his results suggest that an empirical specification similar to that of Carr et al. (2001) is indeed a tractable approach in empirical FDI research. Some other studies find substantial vertical activity going on for certain host countries by using industry-level data (See, for instance, Yeaple 2003, Feinberg and Keene 2001).

A final important issue with the MNE empirical models discussed above is that decisions by MNEs in a source country to invest into a particular host country may be dependent on their FDI decisions to any other host country. This argument is similar to the theory of Anderson (1979) and Anderson and van Wincoop (2003) about the importance of multilateral trade barriers for bilateral trade. There are very few recent studies that allow for interdependence of FDI activity across host countries[9], and some of them apply spatial econometric techniques (Blonigen et al. 2007).

[9]For example, Ekholm et al. (2007) and Yeaple (2003) specify empirical models of export-platform FDI, where a source country invests in a particular host country with the intention of serving third markets with exports of final goods from the affiliate in the host country.

1.2 The study of government architecture

The main functions of the public sector include providing resources in an efficient way, ensuring equity through income distribution, and maintaining macroeconomic and political stability. The proper performance of these tasks depends on the organization of the government (Oates 1972, 1999). The study of the government architecture deals with the question how governments should be organized. The basic organization of governments is being transformed in counties around the world as authority and resources move towards regional and (or) local governments and away from central governments. This shifting of authority from the center to the sub-national levels is what defines decentralization. The purpose of this section is to provide an overview of main benefits and challenges of decentralization in theory and empirics.

Benefits. Traditional economic theories of decentralization emphasize two well-known sources of benefits from decentralization. The best known benefit of decentralized government is the sensitivity of local governments to the varying preferences of their residents (Hayek 1945, Musgrave 1959, Oates 1972). The main argument is that local governments are better able to elicit and make use of local information than the central government. Some citizens may prefer expanded and high-quality programs of public goods, while others may favor smaller public goods provision. By being closer to their constituents the government officials can better reflect the individual tastes and improve the allocation of public spending. This basic argument can be applied to stabilization policy and redistributive policy if the preferences of populations living in different regions are not similar. It also builds the core of the "subsidiarity principle" of decisions introduced to the Maastricht Treaty on the European Union, which means that only those functions should be assigned to the EU center that cannot satisfactorily be fulfilled by the member states. Thus, to the extent that there are heterogenous preferences, Oates' normative policy conclusion is that centralization is costly if it leads the government to provide a bundle of public goods different from the preferences of the citizens of particular regions, provinces, or municipalities.

Tiebout (1956) presents the systematic argument as to how a decentralized government can be used to achieve economic efficiency in the provision of public services. Tiebout (1956) argues that just as competition between firms leads to efficient provision of private goods, so too competition among local communities leads to efficiency in the provision of local public goods. Thus, the second benefit of decentralization is that consumers can reveal their preferences by "voting on foot" as they choose their region of residence where the combination of local public goods and taxes best reflects their preferences; this will force local governments to adapt their public goods provision to the individuals' preferences, if a jurisdiction were to keep its constituents and attract new. In a similar spirit, Brennan and Buchanan (1980) claim that interjurisdictional competition may discipline sub-national governments to reduce corruption and pressure them to supply public goods in an efficient way. Tiebout's argument is also most likely to be behind Brandeis' (1932) statement about local and state governments being "laboratories" for the design of public policy experiments.

The theories presented above have been extended to a political economy setting, with the introduction of transaction costs in the political markets or political agency problems between the politicians/bureaucrats and the electorate. The main argument is that local politicians may be more motivated than national or even provincial politicians, since the former are accountable to the local electorate while the latter have wider constituencies and thus cannot properly response to local issues. Expressed in other words, voters' direct control will be more effective than their indirect control via central representatives (Seabright 1995).

Most of the arguments for decentralization in theory and empirics relate to delivery of public services. Recently, another extension to the traditional theory of decentralization has been made about the role of local governments in promoting local business development. Weingast (1995), Qian and Weingast (1997), and Qian and Roland (1998) argue that decentralization of information and authority and interjurisdictional competition can serve as commitment devices on the part of the central or provincial government to provide market incentives, both positive and negative, the so-called "market preserving federalism"[10].

Challenges. As the World Bank (2000) puts it: "Decentralization itself is neither good nor bad. The issue is whether it is successful or not". First, the main case for decentralization is, as described above, the informational advantage of local governments about residents' preferences and thus their ability to better respond to local needs. However, while the theory is relatively straightforward, the practical case might be less so. The critique is concerned with the incentives and political decision-making on the sub-national and central government tiers. National government officials may be interested to meet local needs, since their reelection depends on the votes of the nation-wide electorate, whereas local governments may happen to have little interest in matching local needs[11] (Tanzi 1995). The problem can be seen from another perspective. Governments are occupied by both politicians and bureaucrats and thus accountability via local elections may come at the cost of accountability via bureaucratic hierarchy and quality. Decentralization transfers authority not only from central to local government officials, but also from central to local bureaucracies. And as Prud'homme (1995) claims, "central government bureaucracies are likely to attract more qualified people [...] because they offer better careers and more possibilities of promotion". Treisman (2007) adds that if all services are assigned to units of the "wrong" scale, this will make a multi-tier provision even more inefficient than unitary provision. Last but not least, some argue that corruption may be more severe on the local level because of the relatively

[10]The market-preserving federalism has been largely considered to be the engine of growth in China in the last two-three decades. In terms of positive incentives, local governments and villages were left to run their own enterprises and "get rich gloriously". In terms of negative incentives, the central government refused to offer inefficient services such as bailouts to bankrupt firms.

[11]This can be the case in both democratic and autocratic regimes, with the situation in the latter being more severe. In the context of developing countries, Bardhan (2002) mentions that the poor and minorities may feel oppressed by the local power groups and look for relief from the national government, which may be able to respond better to their preferences.

greater intimacy and frequency of interaction between local government officials/bureaucrats and citizens (Prud'homme 1995).

Second, the two crucial assumptions of population mobility and perfect interjurisdictional competition in Tiebout's theory may fail in reality turning thus decentralization to be rather challenging than beneficial. Donahue (1997) considers restricted entry and exit in governmental settings, as well as the heterogenous mobility and "citizen's surplus". Graham and Krugman (1989) bring the case for collusion between jurisdictions on the same sub-national tier and argue that "states would be better served if their power to grant investment incentives were simply abolished" (p.119). The reasons for their argument lie in the potential consequences of an intensified interstate bidding for investment, which will be higher taxes and shrunken spending for other constituents and a disproportionate solicitude for more mobile kinds of business.

A different argument about the potential failure of decentralization stemming from Tiebout's competition comes from Inman and Rubinfeld (1997). They argue that when there are significant intercommunity interdependencies, like pure public goods or spillovers, competition among governments results in inefficient public service[12]. Closely related to the previous problem is the case of interregional tax competition for a scarce mobile factor (see, among others, Wilson 1986, 1999; Zodrow and Mieszkowski 1986). The argument is as follows: If a jurisdiction levies too high a tax on its residents' income, capital will flow to another jurisdiction and increase the tax base in the new location. Thus, the taxing region causes a positive fiscal externality to other regions and consequently chooses an inefficiently low level of the externality-producing activity, which is too low tax rates and thus inefficiently low levels of local public goods.

In addition to inter-jurisdictional (horizontal) competition, there exist even greater challenges related to vertical tax competition. A government with multiple layers always means some kind of commonality of tax base between central and sub-national governments (see Keen 1998, Keen and Kotsogiannis 2002, Kessing et al. 2009, Wrede 1997, 2000, among others). The tax imposed by

[12]Examples for such inefficiencies include low income assistance, regulation, and local and business taxes.

one level of government diminishes the size of the tax base available to the other level of government, which will result in a negative externality. The basic problem here is that different levels of government independently tax the same base, and thus tend to overtax.

1.3 Contribution of the thesis

Trade and decentralization. Chapter 2 is a joint work with Sebastian G. Kessing. Increasing globalization of economic activities and decentralization of government organization have been widely observed and debated, but traditionally they have not been linked together. On the one hand, the international trade literature has extensively explored the determinants of and consequences of international trade. On the other hand, the fiscal federalism literature has explored how countries differ in the degree and form in which decision-making powers are allocated across different bodies of government.

Chapter 2 stresses the interaction between the domestic architecture of government and the economic integration with the rest of the world. In particular, it asks empirically how decentralization does affect international and intranational trade. This question is relevant for both trade and public finance economists and policy makers facing ongoing reforms, which change the degree of decentralization in the developed world, and wide-range decentralization programs in the developing world.

The empirical analysis of the chapter is based on a standard gravity model and estimates a sample of 39 countries over a period of twenty years. It differentiates between foreign and domestic trade, where the latter is calculated as the difference between country's gross domestic product and its total exports to the rest of the world. Internal distance has been created following the great circle formula which uses latitudes and longitudes of the most important cities or official capitals. Importer and exporter fixed effects are included as motivated by Anderson and van Wincoop's (2003) multilateral resistance terms. This study makes an important extension to the standard gravity specification by introducing, first, importer and exporter country specific measures of decentralization, and, second, an interaction term between country's degree of decentralization and the home dummy. The last term accounts for the potential impact of decentralization on the willingness to trade domestically rather than internationally, and hence on the home bias. The baseline model together with several robustness specifications have been estimated by the maximum-likelihood Tobit procedure.

The main findings of Chapter 2 can be summarized as follows: Devolution of fiscal responsibilities as measured by the degree of expenditure decentralization plays a significant role on trade. On the one hand, it tends to decrease domestic trade, while on the other hand, it increases both bilateral imports and exports. The reason for the first result is fragmentation of the internal market and the emergence of de facto domestic customs thanks to decentralization. Sub-national governments commonly use their regulatory powers for protective purposes by imposing barriers to movement which makes internal transactions more costly. More expensive intra-country trade itself would make then international transactions relatively more attractive for exporters and importers which accounts for the second result. An alternative potential explanation for the link between decentralization and international trade can be found in the substitute relationship between FDI and foreign trade. Thus, if decentralization diminishes a country's attractiveness as a location for FDI a multinational company would decide to serve the foreign market via exports.

Last but not least, this study may contribute to a better understanding of the magnitude of the "border effect" in international trade. It shows that countries where fiscal decentralization is highest have a two times lower home bias compared to their very centralized counterparts. This result stresses the importance of government structure as additional explanatory variable in the gravity equation.

Foreign direct investment and decentralization. Chapter 3 asks whether countries with centralized governments have a relative advantage to their more decentralized counterparts in the competition for attracting FDI. In particular, how do different forms and degrees of vertical decentralization influence FDI?

This is a relevant question because MNE decisions to service a foreign market through affiliate production depend largely on the way government architecture shapes the investment climate in the targeted location. Specifically, the structure of government has a substantial impact on approaches to taxation and regulation, the provision of infrastructure, the functioning of factor markets, and broader governance features such as corruption, which are all determining factors for FDI.

The formal analysis of the relationship between vertical decentralization and FDI is cast in the empirical KC framework specified in Markusen and Maskus (2002). A sample of 28 source countries, mainly European Union member states, and 19 OECD host countries are considered over the period 1994-2002. The set of KC variables is augmented by different measures of decentralization and the dependent variable is the FDI stock. An important strength of the empirical analysis is the use of a new and improved measure of decentralization, especially fiscal decentralization, which accounts for real tax autonomy by considering only taxes chosen independently and upon which sub-national levels of government have own legislative and administrative powers. The model has been estimated by Tobit in order to account for the numerous zero observations on the side of the dependent variable.

The contribution of this study is twofold. On the one hand, it extends the literature on the empirical determinants of FDI, and, on the other hand, it adds to the numerous well-established applications of the theory on decentralization. Two major results emerge from the analysis of Chapter 3. First, the degree of decentralization in the host country has a robust negative effect on FDI. In particular, the different forms of its vertical dimension tend to reinforce each other and influence the volume of international transactions in a similar detrimental manner. The number of government layers as a measure of the bureaucracy/administrative structure of the government, in general, yields a large and robust negative impact on FDI.

This finding is closely related, among others, to a hold-up hypothesis in the context of FDI. As formulated by Kessing et al. (2007) once an investment is made, some share of it is sunk and irreversible which hinders a firm from moving to another location. In such a situation the government may choose to demand from the investment returns or appropriate the investment completely. The argument emphasizes that the hold-up problem becomes more severe with the increasing number of vertical government layers with which an investor has to deal in a given investment location.

The theoretical literature on decentralization and previous empirical evidence yield mixed results about the effect of the devolution of fiscal powers to sub-national government levels. This chapter, however, finds a consistent negative impact for the degree of tax autonomy and expenditure decentralization as measures of fiscal decentralization. The result can be explained in line with a recent strand of the theoretical literature on tax competition, which emphasizes the inefficiency related to tax and regulatory overlap between the central and sub-national governments. Moreover, the assignment of expenditure and taxing responsibilities in decentralized countries tends not always to be straightforward which creates further coordination challenges in a federated country.

The second outcome is that, though still persistently negative, the effect of fiscal decentralization on FDI tends to assume a U-shaped form. This emerges as a result of the search for an optimal level of decentralization in the context of FDI. The minimum of the function lies at a relatively high rate of tax autonomy, which is present in only four of the sample countries. The most possible explanation for the decreasing intensity of the negative effect of fiscal decentralization after a certain level of decentralization is reached, can be found in the principle of clear separation of powers between the central, regional and local tiers, which precludes inefficiency stemming from common-pool and coordination problems in a decentralized government.

Nation brands and foreign direct investment. Chapter 4 is a joint work with Kai A. Konrad. Whereas the previous chapter shows that FDI is driven by decentralization and other economic and geographic fundamentals, Chapter 4 asks whether intangible factors, such as consumer perceptions about countries and products from these countries, have also an impact on FDI. The question is relevant for shaping government policy and behavior, since government regimes and the way they function determine to a large extent the nation image of a country.

The empirical analysis of Chapter 4 is cast in the KC framework as developed by Carr et al. (2001) and extended by Davies (2008). It is estimated on a sample of 30 source countries and 34 host countries over the short period of 2005-2006. This study is innovative in several ways: First, it investigates a question which has not received attention in the empirical MNE literature. Second, it operationalizes a country's intangibles by its nation brand. Third, it makes an attempt to link insights from marketing theory with international trade empirics.

The concept of the "nation brand" is strongly related to the importance of "country-of-origin" biases for both industrial and consumer products. The "country-of-origin" serves often as a product characteristic, an informational cue, but also as a means of applying a heuristic for simplified decision-making[13]. Given the role the "country-of-origin" may play for purchase decisions, the size and direction of country-of-origin biases should be important for multinational investors when choosing the location of production, and everything else given, investors should choose as their location of production countries to which consumers show a positive country bias. In a similar spirit, nation brands may be used as a heuristic or a source of information about the quality of a country as an investment decision.

These insights lead to the main result of the analysis. The volume of FDI into a host country is shown to rise by 27 percent as its nation image, the value of intangibles, improves by one point. Furthermore, the index carries independent weight in explaining inward FDI flows and is not driven by fundamental or economic variables. The significant and large positive effect of the nation brand index on FDI can serve as important motivation for governments to invest in the improvement of their nation image if they intend to be successful in the competition for attracting FDI.

[13] An elaborate discussion of the related literature can be found in the introductory section to Chapter 4.

Chapter 2

Trade and decentralization

This chapter is joint work with Sebastian G. Kessing from the University of Siegen and CESIfo.

2.1 Introduction

Policy reforms that change the degree of centralization of governance are high on the policy agenda. Countries such as Spain, Belgium, and Great Britain have recently moved to more federal systems, including a substantial devolution of government activities and finances to regional levels. With regards to the developing world, the World Bank and other international policy actors have developed decentralization programs and are actively encouraging countries to decentralize government activities. At the same time, foreign trade has been growing fast, outpacing world output growth more than twice in recent years.[1]

Both developments, rapidly increasing economic integration and political decentralization, have been widely observed and debated. On the one hand, the international trade literature has extensively explored the determinants and consequences of international trade. On the other hand, the fiscal federalism

[1] According to WTO (2006), average trade growth was about six percent over the last decade, whereas average growth of world GDP amounted to less than three percent.

literature has explored how countries differ in the degree and form in which legislative, executive, administrative, and judicial powers are allocated across different bodies of government and considered the optimality of such different institutional arrangements. Traditionally, however, the optimal allocation of government responsibilities across horizontally and vertically distinct government actors has been studied in a closed economy setting, and has hardly considered the implications on international economic transactions. Here, however, we stress the interaction between the domestic architecture of government and the degree of decentralization of government functions, on the one side, and the economic integration with the rest of the world, on the other side. More specifically, the present study directly links decentralization to trade and asks, in particular, how decentralization affects international and intra-national trade.

There are several ways in which decentralization potentially can affect intra-national as well as international trade. First, in decentralized countries multiple governance levels and different jurisdictions on the same sub-national level may introduce rules that lead to fragmentation of the internal market and create *de facto* domestic customs (Tanzi 2000). Of course, natural barriers to intra-national trade - such as transportation costs, ethnic and language diversity - may exist. However, we are concerned about barriers imposed by the government authorities which may lead to inefficient allocation of resources in a fiscal federation. On the one hand, sub-national governments commonly use their regulatory powers for protective purposes by imposing barriers to movement, whether by taxes and subsidies, by regulation, by preferential procurement policies or by the design of local public goods and services[2]. On the other hand, responsibilities within the different government tiers often overlap which results in vertical fiscal externalities (Keen 1998, Keen and Kotsogiannis 2002, Wrede 1997, 2000) if more than one level of government levies regulations on the same project base. These externalities imply that internal transactions should become more costly, as sub-national governments receive more discretion.

[2]Boadway et al. (1994) report, for example, in Brazil the VAT is levied on the state level which creates the potential for differing VAT systems across the country and thus disruption in the internal market.

These potential effects on domestic trade are likely to have important consequences for international trade. As a result of more expensive intra-country trade international transactions can become relatively more attractive for exporters and importers. Such an argument would imply that more decentralized countries are, ceteris paribus, likely to be more prone to export and import to and from other countries relative to their less decentralized counterparts.

Another important channel that links decentralization to a country's international trade is via the relationship between international trade and foreign direct investment (FDI). Firms typically face a trade-off between serving a market via exports, or via establishing an on-site subsidiary through FDI. Recent theoretical and empirical work has shown that decentralization tends to negatively affect FDI. If a foreign investor has dealings with several layers of government, this can create i) problems of rivalry between the different levels, ii) coordination failures, iii) free-riding incentives between government decision makers from different government levels, iv) common pool problems between them when making independent tax and expenditure decisions, v) problems when it comes to the enforcement of implicit contracts between the government and private investors, and vi) moral hazard problems from joint accountability of politicians from different levels and jurisdictions. All these clearly diminish a country's attractiveness as a location for FDI. The federal structure of the host country will thus have a strong influence on FDI, and this view has been supported by the empirical evidence, see, for instance, Kessing et al. (2007) and Kalamova (2008). Thus, if FDI and exports are substitutes we have an additional channel that should relate increased decentralization to increased international trade (and imports, in particular). This line of reasoning would thus suggest a stronger effect of decentralization on imports.

Our analysis considers empirically the role of decentralization measures on the set of bilateral imports of 39 countries, taken from the Directorate of Trade Statistics of the International Monetary Fund. As regressors, we employ the variables used in the standard gravity approach, and the share of sub-national expenditures to total government expenditures - as our major measure of decentralization. We find that the explanatory power of expenditure decentralization is significant and picks up independent weight in the estimation. We show that decentralization decreases domestic trade and increases bilateral trade. The effects are quantitatively more important for the degree of decentralization of the importing country. The findings are robust to a number of alternative specifications. Therefore, we cannot reject our hypotheses about the significant and independent impact of decentralization on both domestic and international trade.

The present study relates to several strands of literature. First, it contributes to the large literature concerned with the determinants of international trade; see, for example, Anderson and van Wincoop (2004) and Jamarchik and Ghosh (2005). We contribute to this literature by regarding decentralization as a *domestic* factor that determines international trade. Furthermore, we build our analysis closely on a growing literature which pays special attention to the 'border' effect, or the so-called home bias[3] and examines the causes of border effects (see, in particular, Chen 2004). Second, some other contributions have considered the interaction of economic integration and the degree of decentralization. This literature has largely focussed on the relationship between decentralization and FDI. In this context it has been argued that the competition between regional governments can reduce the hold-up problem in FDI and create a favorable investment climate (Brennan and Buchanan 1980, Weingast 1995). More recently this view has been challenged by Kessing et al. (2006, 2007) and Kalamova (2008), who argue, and provide empirical evidence, that decentralization negatively affects FDI. Finally, the present study also relates to the work of Alberto Alesina, Enrico Spolaore, and Romain Wacziarg on the size and number of countries; see, for example, Alesina et al. (2000), and Alesina and Spolaore (2003). They also study the relationship between economic integration and political disintegration, but focus on the extreme case of disintegration of government authority: secession. They argue that improved access to world markets reduces the importance of the home market, which results in

[3]This strand of literature was initiated by McCallum (1995), who showed that two Canadian provinces trade 22 times more with each other than with US states of similar size and distance, and many subsequent studies illustrated the negative effect of borders, among others, Helliwell (1996), Wei (1996), Nitsch (2000), Anderson and van Wincop (2003).

higher incentives to break up nations. We return to this direction of causality in our discussion of endogeneity issues in Section 3.

The paper is organized as follows: Section 2 briefly states the main hypotheses. Section 3 describes the data and the econometric methodology implemented. In Section 4 we present the results and Section 5 concludes.

2.2 Hypotheses and empirical strategy

Our theoretical perspective suggests that decentralization will have direct negative impact on domestic trade by imposing internal trade barriers to trade. Furthermore, as a result of more expensive intra-country trade international transactions become relatively more attractive for exporters and importers. And last but not least, considering the substitution between trade and foreign direct investment, the markets of more decentralized countries will be preferably served through goods trade, such that there should be a stronger effect on imports. We state our main conjectures accordingly:

Conjecture 1 *Decentralization directly affects intra-national trade.*

Conjecture 2 *The degree of decentralization of the exporting country affects decisions to export abroad. The effect is likely to be positive.*

Conjecture 3 *The degree of decentralization of the importing country affects incoming international trade flows. The effect is likely to be positive, and potentially stronger than the effect on exports.*

Our empirical strategy is to augment the set of bilateral trade barriers, the common explanatory variables in the trade literature, by exporter and importer-specific measures of 'borders'. For this purpose, we use the degree of expenditure decentralization - the ratio of sub-national government expenditures to total government expenditures - which is the most widely used federalism measure in the literature. This share measure depicts the power distribution between the central government and lower levels of government within a country. We expect this measure to exhibit significant effects on both intra-national and international trade. In particular, we expect higher levels of decentralization in the exporting and importing country to have a negative effect on domestic trade but positive effect on the amount of bilateral trade.

2.3 Data and econometric specification

To test the predictions derived above, our empirical analysis is based on a standard gravity model, which is the most robust device in empirical trade research and is consistent with several theoretical models of trade[4]. Since we are interested in the impact of decentralization on both international and intra-national trade, the dependent variable includes bilateral $Trade_{ij(i \neq j)}$ and domestic $Trade_{ii}$ observations. We obtain bilateral trade data derived from the import side and organized by the 4-digit Standard International Trade Classification from the Direction of Trade Statistics (DOTS) of the International Monetary Fund (IMF). As common in the empirical literature on trade the imports are deflated by the US consumer price index to convert them into real terms (see, for instance, Rose 2004 and Subramanian and Wei 2007). Following other studies[5], we calculate domestic trade for country i as the difference between its gross domestic product and its total exports to the rest of the world. The gravity model considered here takes then the following form:

[4]The theoretical motivation for the gravity framework is found in many general equilibrium models (including Anderson 1979, Bergstrand 1985, Deardorff 1998) in which specialization generates the force of gravity. However, other studies show that the gravity equation can also arise from theories with incomplete specialization and trade costs (Haveman and Hummels 2004, Feenstra et al. 2001, among others). The theoretical foundations for the gravity equation prove to be quite general.

[5]For more detail see Chen (2004), Wei (1996), Nitsch (2000), and Evans (2003), among others.

$$
\begin{aligned}
\ln Trade_{ijt} &= \beta_1 \ln GDP_{it} + \beta_2 \ln GDP_{jt} + \beta_3 \ln Dist \\
&+\beta_4 TradeCosts_{ijt} + \beta_4 Decentral_{it} + \beta_5 Decentral_{jt} \\
&+\beta_6 (Decentral * Domestic)_t + \beta_7 Domestic_t \\
&+\lambda_t + \gamma_i + \gamma_j + c + \varepsilon_{ijt},
\end{aligned}
$$

where *i* and *j* indicate the exporting and importing country, respectively, and *t* the time period. The left-hand side variable $Trade_{ij}$ represents the bilateral trade flow. $Decentral$ denotes the degree of decentralization. $Domestic$ is a dummy variable equal to one for domestic trade $Trade_{ii}$ and to zero for international trade $Trade_{ij(i=j)}$.

The gravity equation in its basic form postulates that the value of trade tends to increase with decreasing international trade barriers between the trading partners and with increasing economic size. Gross domestic product, *GDP*, is our measure for economic size. International borders result from (not) belonging to the same customs union or free trade agreement, (not) sharing common border and same language, or (not) having common colonial history for the exporter-importer pair and are denoted as $TradeCosts_{ij}$: *Customs Union*$_{ij}$, *Free Trade Agreement*$_{ij}$, *Common Border*$_{ij}$, *Common Language*$_{ij}$, and *Common Colony*$_{ij}$.[6] $Dist_{ij}$ denotes bilateral distance between *i* and *j*, and is one of the main explanatory variables in the gravity model by having always proven to be highly significant and robust. International distance here is calculated by following the great circle formula, which uses latitudes and longitudes of the most important cities or official capitals. We build our measure of domestic distance

[6]Each binary variable is equal to 1 when the importing and exporting countries belong to the same customs union or free trade agreement, share the same border and language, and have common colonial history, respectively, and 0 otherwise. Therefore, we expect these variables to enter with a positive sign into our regression. Each of these variables takes a value of zero in the case of domestic trade as in Helliwell (1997). Wei's (1996) way of building the variables by giving them a value of one for domestic trade yields identical results.

by taking a quarter of the distance to the economic center of the nearest trading partner, as suggested in Wei (1996).

Motivated by Anderson and van Wincoop's (2003) multilateral resistance terms[7] we include exporting γ_i and importing country γ_j fixed effects into the estimation. Otherwise, the estimation could lead to biased estimates since relative prices are ignored. Furthermore, we include fixed time effects λ_t to control for omitted, time-variant effects that affect all country-pairs in the same way; c denotes the intercept term and ε_{ijt} is a Gaussian white noise error term.

In Table 2.6 in the Appendix we describe all variables and the sources we collect them from.

The core explanatory variable of our analysis is the level of expenditure decentralization ($Decentral$) - the share of sub-national expenditures in total government expenditures - in both importer and exporter countries. The data come from the IMF's Government Finance Statistics (GFS) and the World Bank Decentralization Database. This measure is the most commonly used in the empirical literature on the effects of fiscal decentralization. Although it is imperfect and cannot capture the differences in the discretion provided to states and local authorities over their fiscal responsibilities, it provides a useful proxy for the relative level of countries' fiscal decentralization. Variations in our measure of expenditure decentralization may result not only from changes in the assignment of competencies between the government levels, but also, and very often, due to business cycle fluctuations. For solving the problem of a spurious relation between decentralization and trade, we calculate four-year-averages for expenditure decentralization. Furthermore, we add the interactive term $Decentral_{i=j} * Domestic$ to the list of regressors, which has a value different from zero only in the cases of domestic trade. Thus, we can account for the impact of decentralization on intra-national trade.

An overview of the values of the expenditure decentralization is presented in Table 2.1. The countries in our sample range from unitary states (for in-

[7]The authors show that, in equilibrium, bilateral trade depends on both exporter and importer price levels, which are themselves functions of trade barriers, the so-called multilateral resistance terms.

Table 2.1: Expenditure decentralization

country	1980-1983	1984-1987	1988-1991	1992-1995	1996-1999
Argentina	29.04	35.71	44.78	43.02	41.40
Australia	40.51	39.77	42.16	42.05	42.62
Austria	30.62	29.85	30.14	31.04	30.89
Bahrain	2.91	2.93	2.78	2.86	2.79
Bolivia		16.27	18.60	18.92	30.43
Brazil	32.45	32.95	33.73	36.16	42.80
Canada	57.83	56.45	55.99	57.18	58.25
Chile	6.87	7.68	9.78	7.60	8.49
Costa Rica	3.44	3.29	3.08	2.77	3.21
Denmark	45.20	43.81	44.67	43.37	45.35
Dominican Republic	3.57	4.56	2.28	2.17	2.64
Finland	38.97	40.20	39.60	34.24	35.62
France	21.85	19.22	17.56	17.65	17.42
Germany	42.50	41.25	40.66	41.30	39.26
Hungary	20.26	20.35	20.40	23.41	23.39
Iceland	25.51	22.40	22.04	23.55	27.04
India	47.43	44.77	44.23	45.69	45.60
Indonesia	11.63	10.55	10.93	12.61	11.86
Ireland	25.11	24.58	22.66	23.64	24.91
Israel	8.88	9.41	12.55	13.81	13.71
Italy		21.34	22.86	20.27	22.60
Malaysia	18.81	19.92	19.67	17.56	18.53
Mauritius	4.30	4.44	4.20	4.71	4.78
Mexico	19.09	14.06	17.43	27.79	28.30
Netherlands	25.57	24.95	23.93	24.34	23.34
Norway	33.09	33.31	33.03	31.75	33.36
Panama	1.91	1.97	2.52	2.46	
Paraguay	5.54	5.33	2.65	2.19	
Philippines	12.02	10.26	7.31	8.70	
Poland		25.21	26.54	16.20	22.86
Portugal		7.23	8.99	11.04	12.41
Romania	19.19	13.16	10.84	10.58	12.64
Spain	14.70	21.79	27.65	30.14	31.69
Sweden	38.68	36.91	36.87	32.54	33.87
Switzerland	53.15	52.05	50.33	48.56	47.29
Thailand	9.69	7.29	7.42	7.65	8.74
United Kingdom	25.09	25.06	25.53	22.57	21.90
United States of America	41.96	42.06	43.92	46.28	47.91
Uruguay	8.62	8.30	10.20	9.95	11.02

Notes: i) The reported values represent four-year averages of the ratio of sub-national expenditures to total expenditures; ii) Data come from the Government Finance Statistics of IMF and the World Bank Decentralization Database.

stance, Bahrain, Costa Rica, and Dominican Republic, among others) with a share of sub-national expenditures in total government expenditures close to zero to the traditional federations like the United States of America, Switzerland, India, Canada, just to mention few of them, where local and regional governments have an equal or higher share of fiscal responsibilities than the central governance level. It is interesting to note, that the level of decentralization remains relatively constant within a large part of the sample. However, we observe some countries (Argentina, Brazil, Mexico and Spain) which have gone through major reforms in the direction of a stronger regional autonomy over the two decades under consideration.

Before turning to our empirical analysis, we should discuss some further methodological issues. Firstly, around 7% of our sample contains zero trade observations. To address this issue we use Tobit estimation which will treat all zero observations as resulting from a censored process. We express the dependent variable as $\ln(Trade_{ijt} + 1)$ in order to contain the zeros in the natural logarithm (see, for example, Chen 2004). Secondly, we build a symmetric set of 39 countries on the exporter and importer sides. As common in the literature, our panel data set consists of observations for every 4 years beginning in 1983 and ending in 1999, which dwindles the time dimension to five periods in total[8]. For expenditure decentralization we use the four-year-averages over the period 1980-1999 rather than just the observations for the years 1983, 1987, 1991, 1995 and 1999. Thirdly, endogeneity is a possible problem, if the value of trade between two countries has an impact on their levels of decentralization. Alesina et al. (2000) have considered the size and number of nations to be determined by the openness of international markets. Decentralization may imply a more gradual step towards a complete secession and, in this view, the

[8]Although the DOTS of IMF, where our dependent variable comes from, covers a wide range of the world trade in goods beyond the period of 1980-1999, we are constrained by the availability of our main explanatory variable, the degree of expenditure decentralization. First, the latter exists for just around eighty countries and, second, a high number of observations are missing for many of those countries along the time dimension. As a result, we include into our analysis all 39 countries, for which there is a coverage over the considered period.

motives towards more decentralization may be seen as analogous to the ones for secession. However, by using period-average-values of decentralization as an explanatory variable and end-of-period trade values on the left hand side, we avoid the potential problem of reverse causality[9].

2.4 Empirical results

We first describe the results for the baseline model. Then we consider the robustness of the results by testing several modifications of the baseline model.

2.4.1 Baseline results

In the baseline specification we regress by Tobit the bilateral import flows on expenditure decentralization of the exporting and importing countries controlling for the standard gravity variables. The first column of Table 2.2 shows the effect of decentralization on domestic trade, the second and third columns account for the direct impact of decentralization on international trade, and the fourth one considers the three effects jointly. Since Tobit coefficients are not directly interpretable, we calculate the marginal effects by the McDonald and Moffit (1980) procedure. Many studies drop the zero observations and estimate trade flows by ordinary least squares (OLS). Therefore, in column (5) we list the results of our baseline specification estimated by OLS. We report only heteroskedasticity-robust standard errors clustered by country-pairs.

We find consistent support for our three main hypotheses, according to which higher decentralization decreases domestic trade but increases international trade. The decentralization coefficients are statistically significant at least at 10% level and enter with the expected signs. The interaction term in column (1) is highly significant and equal to -0.055, suggesting that a one-percent increase in the ratio of sub-national expenditures to total government expenditures

[9]Furthermore, by including the lagged instead of the contemporaneous values of the main explanatory variable - expenditure decentralization - to the regression, we get results about the effect of decentralization on trade, which are similar in sign, magnitude, and explanatory power to the empirical results of the next session.

Table 2.2: Baseline results

Dependent variable: $logTrade_{ij}$					
Variables			**Tobit**		**OLS**
	(1)	**(2)**	**(3)**	**(4)**	**(5)**
logGDP_exp	1.159441***	1.159139***	1.164872***	1.159294***	1.027991***
	(0.1087965)	(0.1088479)	(0.1069404)	(0.1073131)	(0.0982183)
logGDP_imp	0.8418865***	0.8467332***	0.8379126***	0.8348641***	0.6717141***
	(0.1196171)	(0.119409)	(0.1202049)	(0.1207259)	(0.1007025)
logDistance	-0.8757456***	-0.8824698***	-0.8817048***	-0.8738671***	-0.8329626***
	(0.0489934)	(0.0491265)	(0.049082)	(0.0488984)	(0.0441705)
Customs union	0.1163508	0.137915	0.1442317	0.1295307	0.3262652***
	(0.0978006)	(0.099085)	(0.0983891)	(0.0970291)	(0.0882381)
Free Trade Agreement	0.2943366***	0.3245093***	0.3302538***	0.3067001***	0.3487696***
	(0.0965743)	(0.0971294)	(0.0967878)	(0.0962081)	(0.0875661)
Common border	0.4873658***	0.4845002***	0.4837253***	0.4858698***	0.4948414***
	(0.1658684)	(0.1634864)	(0.1634397)	(0.1658421)	(0.1524831)
Common language	0.5112216***	0.4945321***	0.4948302***	0.5122591***	0.4643692***
	(0.1054782)	(0.1056886)	(0.1057033)	(0.1054731)	(0.0970939)
Common colony	0.4934483***	0.5116106***	0.5132338***	0.4964479***	0.4926001***
	(0.1581685)	(0.1571063)	(0.1570585)	(0.1582253)	(0.145365)
Decentralization_exp		0.0069197*		0.0083302**	0.0109922***
		(0.0038201)		(0.0038075)	(0.0035578)
Decentralization_imp			0.0230788***	0.0244865***	0.029699***
			(0.0042609)	(0.0042782)	(0.0041958)
Decentralization∗	-0.055538***			-0.0562753***	-0.0459133***
Domestic	(0.0133738)			(0.0133912)	(0.012667)
Domestic	4.929129***	3.58587***	3.589613***	4.955728***	4.760311***
	(0.4542617)	(0.3534384)	(0.3532477)	(0.4544298)	(0.4297749)
Observations	6973	6973	6973	6973	6499
Uncensored obs.	6499	6499	6499	6499	
(Pseudo) R-squared	0.452	0.448	0.449	0.453	0.901

Notes: i) *** - significant at 1% level, ** - significant at 5% level, * - significant at 10% level; ii) Robust standard errors in parantheses; iii) All estimations include year, exporter and importer dummies; iv) Columns (1)-(4) present Tobit estimates. Column (5) presents OLS results.

will decrease trade within the country by 5.35% (=100*[exp(-0.055)-1]). This result verifies our first hypothesis. At the same time we should ask whether the so-called 'border effect', the willingness to trade rather at home than abroad, is explained by decentralization. For illustration, we compare the border effect in the most decentralized country in our sample (Canada with a value of 58% for expenditure decentralization) with that of a rather centralized country like Indonesia (with 10% decentralization, in average). The coefficients on $Domestic$ and on the interaction term indicate that countries where decentralization is very high have a $Domestic$ coefficient of (4.93-(0.055*58))=1.74, whereas on the contrary more centralized countries have a coefficient of (4.93-(0.055*10))=4.38. These results suggest that higher level of decentralization increases trade abroad by reducing the impact of 'borders', which is an indirect test of hypotheses 2 and 3. We look next at columns (2) and (3) where the direct impact of decentralization on international trade is tested. A one-percentage-point increase in decentralization of the exporting and importing country translates into 0.69% (=100*[exp(0.0069)-1]) and 2.33% (=100*[exp(0.0231]-1) increase in the bilateral trade between them, respectively. The fourth column reinforces the evidence by testing the three hypotheses simultaneously. It also shows that the impact of decentralization in the importing country is quantitatively more important than in the exporting country, in line with our conjecture 3. The OLS estimation in column (5) yields slightly higher coefficients for the decentralization measure in both the exporting and importing countries, which may be due to the omitted zero observations containing information about why low levels of trade are observed. Whether the reported numerical effects are large or modest can be debated, but they are relatively tightly estimated.

In all specifications the gravity explanatory variables are highly significant and display coefficients with the expected signs. The country-specific gross domestic products enter with a positive sign (and their coefficients are close to unity) which verifies the theoretical prediction of the gravity model that the value of trade tends to increase with economic size. Distance has the correct negative coefficient, which means that countries trade more with geographically closer partners. Also the five different proxies for bilateral trade costs have a significant positive sign (except for the customs-union-dummy) as predicted by the theory. For instance, if the partners in a trading pair share the same border, language or colonial history, they will trade above 60%[10] more with each other. Belonging to a free trade agreement also increases bilateral trade. This result is in line with some recent studies. However, the potential impact of the World Trade Organisation and trade agreements on trade flows has become a controversial issue in the trade literature (see, for example, Rose 2004).

2.4.2 Robustness analysis

We begin our robustness analysis by considering an alternative measure of domestic distance. There has been wide debate about the correct measure of domestic distance in the absence of data on actual shipment distances which traces back to Wei (1996), Nitsch (2000), Head and Mayer (2002), and Chen(2004), among others. As previous studies show, the size of the estimated domestic trade bias will be proportional to the value of the average internal distance, which makes the last variable so crucial. We create an alternative measure of domestic distance based on Nitsch (2000), which is equal to the radius of a circle whose area is the area of the country ($r = \sqrt{area}/\sqrt{\pi}$). It becomes obvious from Table 2.3 that the signs and explanatory power of our main regressors, the country-specific decentralization measures, the interaction term and the domestic trade dummy, persist when we use this new distance measure. However, their magnitudes and levels of statistical significance have been slightly affected. The $Domestic$ coefficient here is larger than Wei's measure in Table 2.2 (the same happens in Chen 2004) at the expense of the interaction term, which is smaller now and significant only at 10%. Depending on the specification, countries tend to trade between 80 (=exp(4.41)-1 in columns (2) and (3)) and 160 (=exp(5.10)-1 in columns (1) and (4)) times more at home than abroad. Obviously, the magnitude of the home bias and, thus, of the interaction term is dependent on the choice of the distance measure, whereas the coefficients for $Decentral_i$ and $Decentral_j$ remain unaffected. The current evidence gives us

[10]Common border: 100*[exp(0.487)-1]=62%; Common language: 100*[exp(0.511)-1]=66%; Common colony: 100*[exp(0.493)-1]=64%.

insight into the relative importance of the choice of domestic distance measure, and verifies our baseline results.

There is a reason to suspect that decentralization affects the international trade decisions of developed and developing countries in a different way. It is common knowledge that high-income countries are much more integrated economically with the rest of the world than developing countries are and possess more secure and effective institutions, including federal structures. This fact implies that the level of decentralization in developed economies may be a less determining factor for both import and export decisions in comparison to trade flows incoming or outgoing of a developing country. To account for this we let the country-specific decentralization measures assume potentially different slopes for different combinations of country-pairs. Specifically, we create four dummy variables each equal to one, if both countries in the pair belong to the OECD (*OECDexpOECDimp*), if neither of them belongs to the OECD (*NON-OECDexpNON-OECDimp*), and if one of the trading partners is an OECD member state and the other not (*OECDexpNON-OECDimp* and *NON-OECDexpOECDimp*), respectively, and 0 otherwise. We interact each of this dummies with the sum of the exporting and importing countries' level of decentralization. The results are reported in Table 2.4. In column (1), the negative coefficient in front of the interaction term *Decentral*OECDexpOECDimp* implies that whenever a pair consists of two developed countries the degree of decentralization will be of less concern for their bilateral trade. Columns (3) and (4) indicate in contrast the larger effect of decentralization whenever a non-OECD country is a partner in the trading pair. Although in column (2) the variables keep their magnitudes and significance as in the baseline model, we are surprised by the negative sign in front of the interaction term. Contrary to our assumptions, the degree of decentralization tends to be less important in size when two non-developed countries trade with each other.

In a next step, one can argue that the degree of decentralization should be corrected for some measure of a country size, such as population or area. This would be in line with the insights of Oates (1972) in his classic study of federalism, where the optimal degree of decentralization is related to the size of the

Table 2.3: Alternative distance measure

Dependent variable: $logTrade_{ij}$				
Variables	**(1)**	**(2)**	**(3)**	**(4)**
logGDP_exp	1.16167***	1.15579***	1.16151***	1.161851***
	(0.1082362)	(0.1083713)	(0.1064709)	(0.1067853)
logGDP_imp	0.842848***	0.8412008***	0.8324276***	0.8360926***
	(0.1190312)	(0.1190301)	(0.1198423)	(0.1201071)
logDistance	-0.8746417***	-0.8956948***	-0.8949468***	-0.8723246***
	(0.0482479)	(0.0473642)	(0.0473176)	(0.048178)
Customs union	0.1218311	0.1109691	0.1172791	0.1350166
	(0.0964208)	(0.0961993)	(0.0955117)	(0.0957267)
Free Trade Agreement	0.3169264***	0.3131651***	0.318897***	0.3292016***
	(0.0958594)	(0.0960925)	(0.0957831)	(0.0955573)
Common border	0.4674477***	0.4412434***	0.4404647***	0.4667736***
	(0.1639769)	(0.1616)	(0.1615477)	(0.1639524)
Common language	0.5185767***	0.501155***	0.5014351***	0.5198481***
	(0.1047317)	(0.1042065)	(0.104217)	(0.1047184)
Common colony	0.4862579***	0.5030804***	0.5047238***	0.4888859***
	(0.1604938)	(0.160083)	(0.1600328)	(0.1605171)
Decentralization_exp		0.0068561*		0.0075785**
		(0.0038232)		(0.0038158)
Decentralization_imp			0.0230208***	0.0237184***
			(0.0042632)	(0.0042835)
*Decentralization**	-0.0250497*			-0.0258368*
Domestic	(0.0148613)			(0.0148573)
Domestic	5.072702***	4.411449***	4.414386***	5.100001***
	(0.4681941)	(0.2925819)	(0.2924318)	(0.4685135)
Observations	6973	6973	6973	6973
Uncensored obs.	6499	6499	6499	6499
Pseudo R-squared	0.453	0.452	0.453	0.454

Notes: i) *** - significant at 1% level, ** - significant at 5% level, * - significant at 10% level; ii) Robust standard errors in parantheses; iii) All estimations include year, exporter and importer dummies; iv) All columns present Tobit estimates.

Table 2.4: OECD versus non-OECD countries

Dependent variable: $logTrade_{ij}$				
Variables	**OECDexp OECDimp (1)**	**Non-OECDexp Non-OECDimp (2)**	**Non-OECDexp OECDimp (3)**	**OECDexp Non-OECDimp (4)**
logGDP_exp	1.158975***	1.173491***	1.157675***	1.183662***
	(0.1076437)	(0.1074442)	(0.1069459)	(0.1078705)
logGDP_imp	0.8318344***	0.8484118***	0.845564***	0.8288078***
	(0.1207951)	(0.1210247)	(0.1207254)	(0.1211941)
logDistance	-0.8900182***	-0.8812778***	-0.8822569***	-0.8912783***
	(0.0491013)	(0.0492097)	(0.0493421)	(0.0489214)
Customs union	0.2040861**	0.1836629*	0.1757469*	0.2247115**
	(0.0947431)	(0.0972321)	(0.0953491)	(0.0953623)
Free Trade Agreement	0.374131***	0.3316214***	0.3398329***	0.3742897***
	(0.0957286)	(0.0950802)	(0.0954629)	(0.0948699)
Common border	0.4997122***	0.5021307***	0.4967079***	0.5082944***
	(0.1632712)	(0.1657694)	(0.1646991)	(0.1639307)
Common language	0.5278397***	0.5054708***	0.5152163***	0.518541***
	(0.1036071)	(0.1052369)	(0.1044388)	(0.1039019)
Common colony	0.4949201***	0.4990624***	0.4968833***	0.4972951***
	(0.1549341)	(0.1574192)	(0.15663)	(0.1553847)
Decentralization_exp	0.0109626***	0.0084104**	0.0085412**	0.0051958
	(0.0038126)	(0.0037852)	(0.0037844)	(0.003985)
Decentralization_imp	0.0271024***	0.0245216***	0.0229486***	0.0248766***
	(0.0043728)	(0.0042461)	(0.0043012)	(0.0043429)
Decentralization∗	-0.0045662***			
OECDexpOECDimp	(0.0013747)			
Decentralization∗		-0.0043935*		
Non-OECDexpNon-OECDimp		(0.0022949)		
Decentralization∗			0.0032194**	
Non-OECDexpOECDimp			(0.0015631)	
Decentralization∗				0.0066556***
OECDexpNon-OECDimp				(0.0016875)
Decentralization∗	-0.0541491***	-0.0541773***	-0.0547526***	-0.0531424***
Domestic	(0.013373)	(0.0133777)	(0.0133769)	(0.013368)
Domestic	4.933777***	4.916104***	4.933425***	4.909769***
	(0.4558623)	(0.4537817)	(0.4546208)	(0.4540891)
Observations	6973	6973	6973	6973
Uncensored obs.	6499	6499	6499	6499
Pseudo R-squared	0.454	0.453	0.453	0.455

Notes: i) *** - significant at 1% level, ** - significant at 5% level, * - significant at 10% level; ii) Robust standard errors in parantheses; iii) All estimations include year, exporter and importer dummies; iv) All columns present Tobit estimates.

country in terms of population[11]. To control for that we add population and area into our estimation. Columns (1)-(3) in Table 2.5 clearly show that the inclusion of these additional control variables does not change our previous results. The decentralization coefficients retain their magnitudes and levels of statistical significance as in the baseline specification.

It is interesting to check whether the results reported above are dependent on our measure of decentralization, the ratio of sub-national expenditures to total government expenditures. For this purpose we introduce alternative measures of decentralization to our baseline specification. First, we use the share of sub-national revenues in total government revenues which also comes from the GFS of IMF. According to this variable the most decentralized country in our sample is Canada with an average of 53% revenue decentralization, while the Dominican Republic is among the most centralized countries with less than 1% revenue powers on the sub-national level. In many countries the practice of federalism has been witnessing large discrepancies between the revenue and expenditure discretionary powers, leading to strong dependence of the sub-national governments on the central government revenues to support their expenditures, the so-called vertical imbalances. However, in our sample these two forms of fiscal decentralization seem to be highly correlated. It becomes obvious from columns (4)-(5) in Table 2.5 that revenue decentralization yields very similar results, in size and magnitude, to the baseline model which uses expenditure decentralization.

---

[11]"One important factor influencing the extent of centralization should be the size of the nation in terms of population [...] In a relatively small country, for example, there are likely to be real cost-savings in centralizing a substantial portion of the activity in the public sector. As a nation becomes larger, however, it becomes efficient for decentralized jurisdictions, because of their own significant size, to provide their own outputs of a wide range of public services. Moreover, as a country grows in size, central administration becomes more difficult and is likely to result in a less effective use of resources within the public sector. For these reasons we would expect the degree of fiscal centralization to vary inversely with the size of a country." (Oates 1972, pp. 200–1)

Table 2.5: Alternative measures of decentralization

Dependent variable: $logTrade_{ij}$							
Variables	**Expenditure decentralization**			**Revenue decentralization**		**Government tiers**	
	(1)	**(2)**	**(3)**	**(4)**	**(5)**	**(6)**	**(7)**
logGDP_exp	1.308347***	1.159294***	1.308347***	1.19221***	1.372093***	0.8800303***	1.005743***
	(0.1192769)	(0.1073131)	(0.1192778)	(0.1098772)	(0.1229562)	(0.0185763)	(0.026105)
logGDP_imp	0.8352742***	0.8348641***	0.8352742***	0.8744295***	0.8785219***	0.8209593***	0.9658068***
	(0.1381499)	(0.1207259)	(0.1381509)	(0.1218703)	(0.140962)	(0.0179563)	(0.0268802)
logDistance	-0.8754685***	-0.8738671***	-0.8754685***	-0.8878065***	-0.8895523***	-0.767924***	-0.6783472***
	(0.0489956)	(0.0488984)	(0.0489959)	(0.0499436)	(0.0499953)	(0.0475052)	(0.0522199)
Customs union	0.1157437	0.1295307	0.1157437	0.1217221	0.103561	0.5091757***	0.3174881***
	(0.0986168)	(0.0970291)	(0.0986175)	(0.1014697)	(0.1033259)	(0.0981389)	(0.1011312)
Free Trade Agreement	0.2975369***	0.3067001***	0.2975369***	0.3145024***	0.3033083***	0.4379452***	0.3279653***
	(0.0968492)	(0.0962081)	(0.09685)	(0.0975797)	(0.0983373)	(0.1005411)	(0.1027148)
Common border	0.4868673***	0.4858698***	0.4868673***	0.4556415***	0.4572126***	0.6922771***	0.8954674***
	(0.1655842)	(0.1658421)	(0.1655855)	(0.1662467)	(0.1658657)	(0.1394055)	(0.1700277)
Common language	0.5117823***	0.5122591***	0.5117823***	0.4972967***	0.4960997***	0.3229234***	0.3881401***
	(0.1054671)	(0.1054731)	(0.1054679)	(0.1076027)	(0.1075705)	(0.1068484)	(0.1018351)
Common colony	0.4954809***	0.4964479***	0.4954809***	0.5092857***	0.5084256***	0.597397***	0.4475192**
	(0.1582503)	(0.1582253)	(0.1582514)	(0.1609393)	(0.1609461)	(0.1923556)	(0.1889492)
logPopulation_exp	-0.6472146**		-0.6472146**		-0.7764779***		-0.2021555***
	(0.2845804)		(0.2845825)		(0.2902609)		(0.0356918)
logPopulation_imp	-0.0162217		-0.0162217		-0.036131		-0.17489***
	(0.284781)		(0.2847831)		(0.2951173)		(0.0346158)
logArea_exp		-0.2062508**	0.2942143		0.3848431*		-0.0103547
		(0.0855738)	(0.2237667)		(0.2281732)		(0.022876)
logArea_imp		-0.104432	-0.222146		-0.1689658		-0.0700018***
		(0.0938185)	(0.2209895)		(0.2285437)		(0.0221548)

Table 2.5 continued: Alternative measures of decentralization

Variables	Expenditure decentralization			Revenue decentralization		Government tiers	
	(1)	(2)	(3)	(4)	(5)	(6)	(7)
Decentralization_exp	0.0099326**	0.0083302**	0.0099326**				
	(0.0038371)	(0.0038075)	(0.0038371)				
Decentralization_imp	0.0244948***	0.0244865***	0.0244948***				
	(0.0043196)	(0.0042782)	(0.0043196)				
*Decentralization**	-0.0563187***	-0.0562753***	-0.0563187***				
Domestic	(0.0134034)	(0.0133912)	(0.0134035)				
Revenue decentralization_exp				0.0088439**	0.0115243***		
				(0.0042898)	(0.0043208)		
Revenue decentrallization_imp				0.0181754***	0.0182449***		
				(0.0052163)	(0.0052873)		
*Revenue decentralization**				-0.0478893***	-0.0479214***		
Domestic				(0.0159854)	(0.0160044)		
Government tiers_exp						0.1042543**	0.306309***
						(0.0461548)	(0.0559472)
Government tiers_imp						0.0957766**	0.313827***
						(0.0440633)	(0.0517978)
*Government tiers*Domestic*						-0.3005763**	-0.2945902*
						(0.1425001)	(0.154034)
Domestic	4.948618***	4.955728***	4.948618***	4.403261***	4.394538***	6.108736***	6.407881***
	(0.4542729)	(0.4544298)	(0.4542763)	(0.4674423)	(0.4673973)	(1.04557)	(1.094342)
Observations	6973	6973	6973	6748	6748	6673	6673
Uncensored obs.	6499	6499	6499	6285	6285	6204	6204
Pseudo R-squared	0.453	0.453	0.453	0.450	0.45	0.379	0.389

Notes: i) *** - significant at 1% level, ** - significant at 5% level, * - significant at 10% level; ii) Robust standard errors in parantheses; iii) All estimations include year, exporter and importer dummies; iv) All columns present Tobit estimates.

As a second alternative measure of decentralization we use a variable counting the number of government tiers in a country. It has been constructed by Treisman (2002) and takes discrete values between 1 and 6, where most of the countries in our sample are assigned 3-4 tiers. This variable is a good proxy for the number of decision makers in a federation, which we cannot capture by our measures of fiscal decentralization. However, since it is time invariant we drop the country fixed effects from the estimation, but still keep the time dummies. Column (6) reports the results for government tiers only and column (7) controls for demographic size. A one-tier increase in both exporting and importing countries results into a 10%-35% growth in bilateral trade. The impact on domestic trade expressed by the interaction term between decentralization and the home dummy seems to be similar in magnitude, but negative in sign, as expected. This variable has a much larger effect on trade than our measures of fiscal decentralization, which results to a great extent from its nature. A federalism reform which adds a government level to the federal structure of a country may translate into more than 10% increase in fiscal decentralization[12] and thus reach the same statistical effect.

2.5 Concluding remarks

In this paper, we use the theory-based gravity model to investigate the effects of decentralization on trade. The approach has been augmented by allowing for measures of decentralization to affect both domestic and international trade. The share of sub-national expenditures to total government expenditures has been our major measure of decentralization. We find that the explanatory power of expenditure decentralization is significant and picks up independent weight in the estimation. We show that decentralization decreases domestic trade and increases bilateral trade. The findings are robust to a number of alternative specifications. From a theoretical perspective, our results are in line with a picture of decentralization that makes domestic trading relatively less favorable due

[12]Countries like Spain and Mexico which have gone through major federalism reforms are good examples, where the inclusion of one more government level has led to a significant jump in the degree of fiscal decentralization.

to fragmentation of the internal market and fiscal and regulatory externalities. This results in a substitution of domestic trading by international transactions. An alternative link exists in the substitute relationship between foreign direct investment and foreign trade.

2.6 Appendix

Table 2.6: Data sources

Variables	Description
Trade	Bilateral import data in US dollars from the Directorate of Trade Statistics of the International Monetary Fund (IMF). We convert the variable into real terms by deflating it with the US consumer price index from the International Financial Statistics of the IMF; Domestic trade is calculated as the difference between GDP of the country and its exports to the rest of the world; Own calculations.
GDP	Gross domestic product of exporter and importer in constant US dollars with base year 2000; Source: World Development Indicators (WDI).
Distance	Bilateral distance in km between the capitals of the exporting and importing country; Source: Centre d'Etudes Prospectives et d'Informations Internationales (CEPII); Domestic distance is calculated as a quarter of the distance to the economic center of the nearest trading partner following Wei (1996); Own calculations
Common Language	A binary variable equal to 1 if the country-pair shares the same language and 0 otherwise; Source: CEPII.
Customs Union	A binary variable equal to 1 if the country-pair belongs to the same customs union and 0 otherwise; Source: World Trade Organization (WTO), own compilation.
Free Trade Agreement	A binary variable equal to 1 if the country-pair belongs to the same free trade agreement and 0 otherwise; Source: WTO, own compilation.
Common Border	A binary variable equal to 1 if the country pair shares the same border and 0 otherwise; Source: CEPII.
Common Colony	A binary variable equal to 1 if the country pair shares the same colonial history and 0 otherwise; Source: CEPII.
Population	Number of citizens in each country; Source: WDI.
Area	Surface area in square meters for each country; Source: CEPII.

Expenditure decentralization	Ratio of sub-national government expenditures to total government expenditures with a range between 0 and 100; Source: Government Finance Statistics (GFS) of IMF and World Bank Decentralization Database.
Revenue decentralization	Ratio of sub-national government revenues to total government revenues with a range between 0 and 100; Source: GFS of IMF and World Bank Decentralization Database.
Tiers	A discrete varable between 1 and 6 equal to the number of central and sub-central government levels; Source: Treisman (2002).

Chapter 3

Foreign direct investment and decentralization

3.1 Introduction

Multinational enterprise activity in the form of foreign direct investment (FDI) has grown at a faster rate than most other international transactions, particularly trade flows between countries. The decisions of multinational enterprises (MNEs) to service a foreign market through affiliate production depend largely on the way government architecture shapes the investment climate in targeted locations. While governments have limited influence on factors such as geography, they have more decisive influence on approaches to taxation and regulation, the provision of infrastructure, the functioning of factor markets, and broader governance features such as corruption. This paper focuses on one aspect of the structure of government - decentralization - and its impact on FDI, in particular.

Decentralization means a multi-level government. It is defined as the devolution of authority from the central government towards the sub-national government levels. Research in this area has distinguished between two different dimensions: horizontal and vertical. The horizontal dimension deals with the division of sub-national government tiers into mutually exclusive territorial units, such as states, regions, counties, etc. It is usually associated with inter-jurisdictional competition for mobile capital and the positive externality of low tax burden stemming from that (see Wilson 1999 for an overview of the literature on tax competition). The vertical dimension is concerned with the optimal number of government tiers to be found in a country below the center and the interdependencies between them. Recent literature relates this aspect to the fact that decentralization makes the economic agents subject to several vertically differentiated government levels, which translates into a commonality problem.

In the context of FDI, I consider that once an investment takes place in a particular location, the market and political conditions of the surrounding jurisdictions do not matter any more because of the fixed costs associated with establishing the investment project and their irreversibility. What matters for the success of the investment is the structure of government and the quality of its policy and bureaucracy on the different hierarchical levels which are responsible for the particular investment location. The present study is thus concerned with the vertical dimension of decentralization and asks how different forms and degrees of this dimension do influence FDI.

Several theoretical arguments can be brought forward to explain the relationship between vertical decentralization and inward FDI. First, a government with multiple layers means some commonality of the tax base between central and sub-national governments as stressed by Keen (1998), Keen and Kotsogiannis (2002), Kessing et al. (2009), and Wrede (1997, 2000). The co-existence of central and regional corporate income taxes and/or local business taxes is the common praxis in the developed world. A tax base overlap, no matter whether it is perfect or a less strong variant always leads to inefficiency. The basic problem is that when local and central governments can independently tax the same base or are expected by voters to spend on the same items, they tend to overtax or underspend.

Second, the arguments about the higher level of taxation in countries with a larger number of government layers can equally apply to governmental regulatory quality and corruption, in particular. If the separate layers of government do not collude, their aggregate extraction of bribes will be higher than that of an equally predatory unitary government (Shleifer and Vishny 1993). Moreover, Kessing et al. (2006) show that a collusive outcome is, in general, more difficult in countries with higher number of autonomous tiers, which increases the likelihood of a hold-up problem in the context of FDI[1].

Third, governments are occupied by both politicians and bureaucrats and there are two potential problems related to that. Some argue that multi-tier governments are likely to duplicate each other and waste resources. As Rousseau (1762) puts it, "[administration] becomes more burdensome as the chain of command is lengthened". The second problem is that central government bureaucracies are likely to attract more qualified people and corruption may be more severe on the local level because of the relative proximity between local government officials/bureaucrats and economic agents (Prud'homme 1995).

Fourth, the assignment of expenditure and taxing responsibilities in decentralized countries is not always straightforward. Treisman (2007) points out that in case of increasing local governments' shares the local governments become more motivated to support economic performance, whereas the central level of government may become less motivated since its share in the general government decreases. This may lead to low public service and high regulations levied by the center, and to a poor infrastructure, in general. However, since all levels of government can influence economic performance and the local government level with its higher share may compensate for the activity of the national level, the resulting net effect on performance is indeterminate.

The last argument adds to the responsibility-sharing problem discussed above. In the case of equally important players, or in other words, when the subnational and the central levels have equal shares of the general government, and clearly defined responsibilities, there will be transparency about the general regulatory framework[2]. This may reverse the effect of decentralization on

---

[1]The hold-up problem in the context of FDI emerges as a result of time-inconsistent government policy. The main idea is that capital moves freely only until investment is made in a selected location. Then the host government can opt for a change in its tax policy in a predatory manner. This extractive behavior, once anticipated by the foreign investor, will have a negative effect on the investment decisions. (Kessing et al. 2007)

[2]I refer to the literature on vertical fiscal externalities and practical evidence from the World Bank (2000),

FDI and thus make a more vertically decentralized country more attractive for investors.

Despite the numerous theoretical arguments about the interaction between the domestic government architecture and the economic integration with the rest of the world few empirical studies have scrutinized this relationship. Kessing et al. (2007) make an insightful contribution to this topic by testing a causal link between the degree of decentralization and FDI. In particular, they investigate whether the vertical government structure has a direct effect on FDI as predicted by the theory. For this purpose, bilateral cross-border acquisitions are regressed on several measures of decentralization. Their results point at a detrimental effect of vertical decentralization associated with the number of sub-national government tiers, on the one side. On the other side, devolution of fiscal responsibilities to lower levels of government tends to affect FDI positively. The study of Kessing et al. (2007) features some limitations related mainly to the data used. The present paper extends the analysis about the impact of decentralization on FDI by developing further hypotheses, employing a more sophisticated empirical approach and using different data for FDI and improved decentralization measures.

My formal analysis of the relationship between vertical decentralization and FDI is cast in the empirical KC framework specified in Markusen and Maskus (2002). A sample of 28 source countries, mainly European Union member states, and 19 OECD host countries are considered over the period 1994-2002. The set of KC variables is augmented by different measures of decentralization and the dependent variable is the FDI stock from EUROSTAT. An important strength of the empirical analysis is the use of a new and improved measure of decentralization, especially fiscal decentralization, which accounts for real tax autonomy by considering only taxes chosen independently and upon which sub-national levels of government have own legislative and administrative powers. The contribution of this study is twofold. On the one hand, it extends the literature on the empirical determinants of FDI (for an overview see Blonigen 2005), and, on the other hand, it adds to the numerous well-established applications of the theory on decentralization. Two major results emerge from the analysis.

First, the degree of decentralization in the host country has a robust negative effect on FDI. In particular, the different forms of its vertical dimension tend to reinforce each other and influence the volume of international transactions in a similar detrimental manner. The number of government layers as a measure of the administrative structure of government yields a large and robust negative impact on FDI. Furthermore, I find a consistent negative impact for fiscal decentralization. The second outcome is that, though still persistently negative, the effect of fiscal decentralization on FDI tends to assume a U-shaped form.

The paper is organized as follows. In section 2 I present briefly the main hypotheses. Section 3 discusses the measures of decentralization which fit best as a test for the hypotheses. Section 4 describes the econometric approach and the data and Section 5 - the empirical results. Section 6 concludes.

3.2 Testable hypotheses

My central argument maintains that by decentralizing general administration and delegating decision-making rights to local or state governments, vertical decentralization makes an MNE subject to several government tiers at the same time. The different tiers independently levy taxes, impose regulations and provisions, or charge certain fees on the investment project in order to increase tax revenues. These policy instruments add additional financial and administrative burden for the investor. Moreover, overlapping responsibilities on the expenditure side may result into poor provision and quality of public service and infrastructure. All these factors impose extra "costs" on the firms and thus affect their decision to invest and extend an investment project in a particular location. The first main conjecture claims that:

Conjecture 1 *Vertical decentralization of the host country negatively affects incoming FDI.*

However, once the different levels of government have received relatively similar shares in the decision-making of the country and have clearly assigned taxing and expenditure powers, the effect of decentralization on FDI will reverse. This means that a certain threshold exists beyond which an increase in the amount of vertical decentralization will have a positive effect on incoming FDI. Based on this argument I can derive the second main conjecture:

Conjecture 2 *A U-shaped relationship between vertical decentralization and FDI may exist.*

3.3 Measuring decentralization

Most of the theoretical arguments introduced above relate to the vertical coordination challenges in the public sector, while the rest draw implications about the vertical administrative structure of government, in general. Thus, to account for the validity of the hypotheses, I split the vertical dimension of decentralization into its fiscal and bureaucracy/administrative components resulting from the hierarchical structure of the multi-level government. Fiscal decentralization reflects how responsibilities for tax revenues and public expenditures are distributed among different tiers of government, whereas administrative decentralization is present when each sub-national tier has "at least one area of action in which it is autonomous" (Riker 1964, p.11). For the latter form of decentralization, it makes little difference whether decision-makers at a particular government tier are appointed or elected (Oates 1972). Treisman (2007, pp. 21-27) provides an elaborate discussion of the different patterns of decentralization[3].

First, a more fiscally decentralized state will be one in which lower level governments have greater autonomy to define their tax bases, set their own tax rates, and determine their own public spending. Shifts in the degree of fiscal decentralization are either due to changes in the vertical allocation of functions

[3]In particular, Treisman (2007) differentiates between forms of decentralization i) where government officials at one or more sub-national tiers are selected by local residents versus appointed by the central government directly, and ii) where at least one sub-national tier of government has authority to make decisions on at least one policy issue versus sub-national governments have a formal right to participate in central policymaking. For illustration, fiscal decentralization, as defined in this paper, is clearly a form of decisionmaking decentralization (on tax and expenditure issues), while appointment decentralization (also the electability of government officials at one or more tiers by local residents) accounts for the bureaucracy/administrative structure of the multi-level governance.

or in the relative demand for certain public goods. Thus, without taking into account the vertical structure of decision-making, the degree of decentralization of the public sector tends to be misrepresented (Oates 1972). For this reason, a reliable measure of fiscal decentralization needs to effectively quantify the activities of sub-national governments arising from their autonomous decisions. The standard approach in the literature is to use accounting measures from the Government Finance Statistics (GFS) at the International Monetary Fund (IMF) of the share of sub-national government revenue (or expenditure) in consolidated general government revenue (or expenditure) as a proxy for the degree of decentralization in the public sector, although it is widely accepted that budgetary data are imperfect indicators of the actual degree of fiscal decentralization[4].

Recently, Stegarescu (2005) overcomes the major problems related to the revenue side of decentralization by creating a corrected indicator of tax revenue decentralization following the methodology in OECD (1999). This variable accounts only for taxes chosen independently and upon which sub-central levels of government have own legislative and administrative powers[5]. As a principal measure of vertical fiscal decentralization I use Stegarescu's tax revenue decentralization variable, which reflects the share of discretionary tax revenues over general government revenues expressed as a percentage and is available only for several OECD member countries. Table 3.1 shows that Ireland appears to be the most fiscally centralized country in the sample with a share of only

[4]Until recently, the GFS variables have been the only existent time-series data generating measures for expenditure and revenue decentralization. However, these variables have often been criticized of misrepresenting the true nature of decentralization, since they cannot capture the differences in the discretion provided to states and local authorities over their fiscal responsibilities. First, these shares represent expenditure and revenue figures at the different government levels which ultimately operate or receive them, irrespective of whether they have discretion upon the fiscal activities. It is therefore difficult to interpret them as indicators of fiscal autonomy. Second, they also fail to capture the legislative and regulatory activities and other aspects of vertical decentralization in the public sector. For further discussion of the main limitations of these indicators look at Stegarescu (2005).

[5]For creating the indicator only taxes are considered for which according to the OECD (1999) classification the sub-central government determines i) both, base and tax rate, ii) tax rate only, iii) tax base only.

2.4% and Switzerland the most decentralized country with a 54.8% share of autonomous sub-national to total tax revenues in average. In contrast to what one expects for a traditional federal country and what GFS predicts, the degree of tax decentralization amounts to only 7.2% for Germany according to the OECD methodology compared to 49.6% when considering all sub-central government tax revenues. While the current data represent a major improvement of the existing revenue decentralization indicator, the measurement flaws on the expenditure side of decentralization have still not been resolved. As a robustness check, I use the standard GFS sub-national expenditure share collected from the World Bank Decentralization Database as a proxy for vertical expenditure decentralization. Regardless of the OECD methodology, Stegarescu's tax decentralization is in average correlated up to 70% with the GFS measure of expenditure decentralization (compare Table 3.11). Although the joint effect of these two variables would be interesting to observe, the inclusion of both into the same regression equation may lead to multicollinearity. To avoid this potential problem I create a factor variable comprised by equal shares of the expenditure and corrected tax revenue decentralization measures and use it in the econometric analysis.

Second, a government which is administratively decentralized appoints officials (bureaucrats) in lower tier jurisdictions to implement at least one policy. This form of decentralization accounts for vertical competition and coordination problems stemming from other factors than fiscal externalities. To express the bureaucracy structure of government as a specific feature of decentralization I use the number of government tiers in the host country. This variable has been recently created by Daniel Treisman who defines a tier as follows: "A level of territorial subdivision of the state is said to constitute a tier if: 1) subdivisions at this level have an executive with government authority; 2) this executive has responsibility for general administration, not just provision of a particular public service; and 3) the superior tier of government (or, for first-tier units, the entire state) is subdivided territorially into units of this type (at least in some areas). The definition of a tier applies equally to governments with or without legislative councils, and with or without elected leaders, and so includes

Table 3.1: Measures of decentralization

Host country	**Tax decentralization**	**Expenditure decentralization**	**Government tiers**
Australia	21.38	42.33	3
Austria	3.52	30.93	4
Belgium	23.76	11.07	4
Canada	52.96	57.70	4
Denmark	31.63	44.71	3
Finland	26.68	34.75	3
France	19.41	17.54	4
Germany	7.17	39.92	4
Ireland	2.44	24.43	3
Italy	7.71	22.13	4
Netherlands	4.96	23.62	3
New Zealand	5.60	10.44	3
Norway	23.61	32.81	3
Portugal	3.00	11.84	
Spain	18.75	30.90	4
Sweden	44.47	33.00	3
Switzerland	54.79	47.68	3
United Kingdom	4.89	22.11	4
United States of America	36.90	47.49	4

Notes: i) Averages over the sample period are reported for tax and expenditure decentralization; ii) Data on tax decentralization has been provided by Stegarescu (2005), Expenditure decentralization has been collected from the World Bank Decentralization Database, while Government tiers - from Treisman (2002).

Figure 3.1: Decentralization and log of FDI to GDP

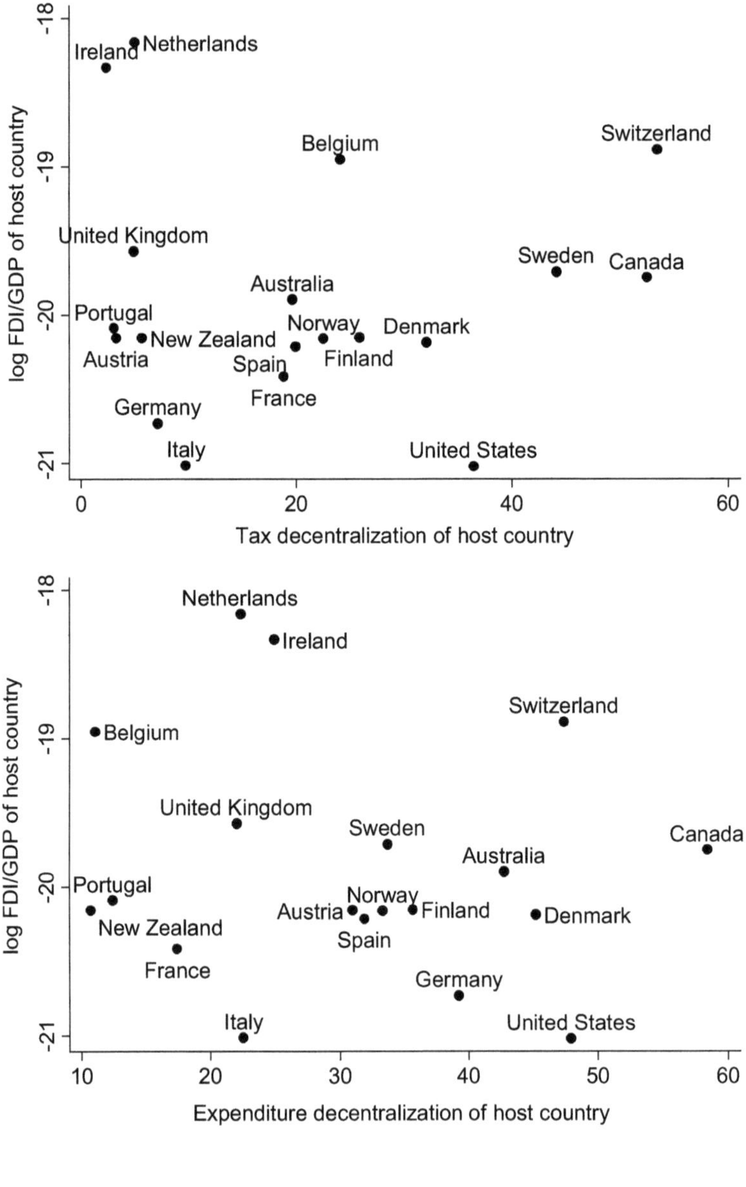

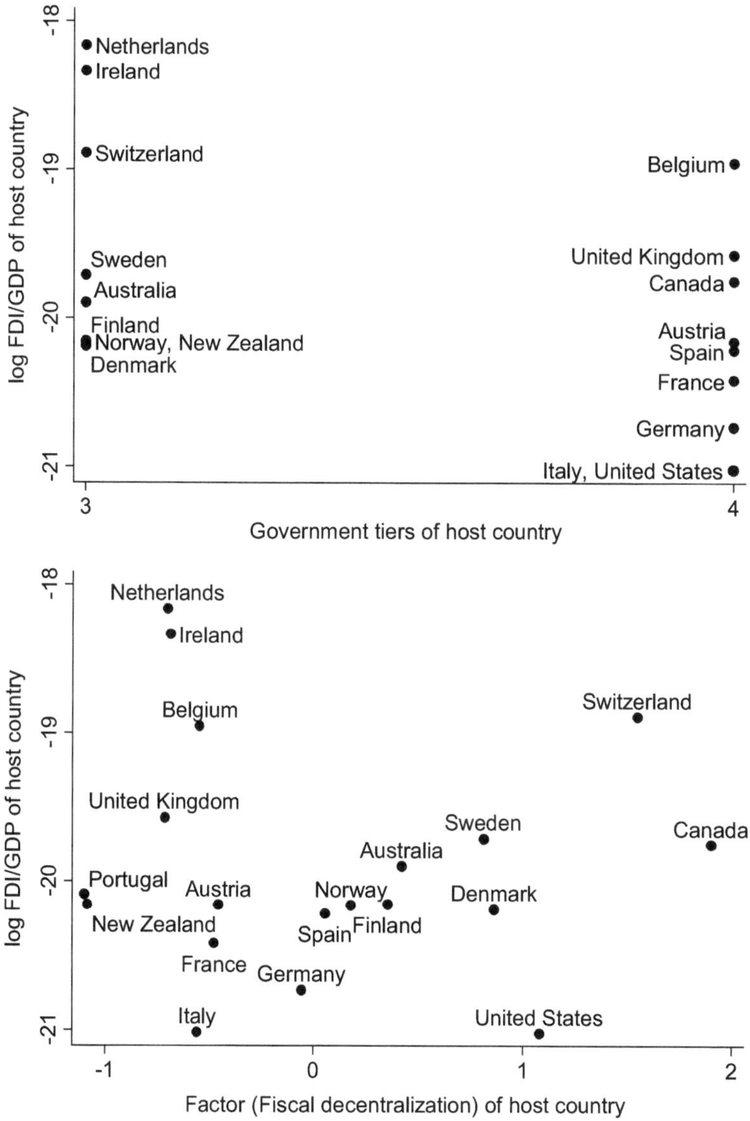

-18
-19
-20
-21
log FDI/GDP of host country
Netherlands
Ireland
Switzerland
Sweden
Australia
Finland
Norway, New Zealand
Denmark
Belgium
United Kingdom
Canada
Austria
Spain
France
Germany
Italy, United States
3
4
Government tiers of host country
-18
-19
-20
-21
log FDI/GDP of host country
Netherlands
Ireland
Belgium
Switzerland
United Kingdom
Sweden
Canada
Australia
Portugal
Austria
Norway
Denmark
New Zealand
Spain
Finland
France
Germany
Italy
United States
-1
0
1
2
Factor (Fiscal decentralization) of host country

what are often termed levels of administration" (Treisman 2002). In general, the variable can take values between 1 and 6, whereas all of the countries in my sample are assigned 3 or 4 tiers. Table 3.1 shows, for example, that although Ireland is the most centralized country according to Tax decentralization, it appears to be similar in its administrative structure to a typical federal country like Switzerland. This points out that a decentralized government per se does not necessarily imply fiscal decentralization (see also Arzaghi and Henderson 2005).

Last, Figure 3.1 plots the decentralization measures against the log of total FDI stock in each host country relative to its gross domestic product. All variables are averaged over the period of consideration in this work. A negative relationship between decentralization and FDI can be clearly identified. Concerning fiscal decentralization three traditional federated countries, Canada, Switzerland and USA, seem to be outliers at the right end of the distribution with their large degrees of decentralization.

3.4 Data and econometric specification

To assess the predictions about the impact of vertical decentralization on FDI, I base my empirical analysis on the knowledge-capital (KC) model of Carr. et al. (2001) and Markusen and Maskus (2002), augmenting the set of variables by the different measures of decentralization described above. The KC model serves explaining the volume of production of multinational companies abroad and real affiliate sales would be the preferable measure of FDI activity, since it captures the value of multinational activity and helps to control for differences in the technology across firms. However, the only commonly available data are for the United States. To cover a broad range of source and host countries I use as a dependent variable the position of foreign direct investment from the European Union Direct Investment Yearbook by EUROSTAT reported from the source country side. Blonigen et al. (2003) among others identify the real FDI stock as a suitable proxy for affiliate production, which validates the choice of my dependent variable. To transform the data into real values I deflate the series by the US gross domestic product deflator with base year 2000 (which is the standard in the literature). The EUROSTAT data set suits well my empirical strategy of examining the pattern of international capital movements within the OECD area not only due to its broad availability but also because national data have been harmonized which makes a cross-section comparison possible, and missing and zero observations are differentiated. 28 source countries[6] are considered here, while the set of host countries comprises 19 OECD member states[7]. I estimate a regression equation of the following form:

$$
\begin{aligned}
FDI_{ijt} \quad = \quad & c + \beta_1 \sum GDP_{(i,j)t} + \beta_2 \left(\Delta GDP_{(i,j)t}\right)^2 + \beta_3 INT1_t \\
& + \beta_4 INT2_t + \beta_5 INT3_t + \beta_6 Dist_{ij} + \beta_7 TradeCosts_{ijt} \\
& + \beta_8 Tariff f_{it} + \beta_9 Tariff f_{jt} + \beta_{10} INVC_{jt} + \beta_{11} Governance_{jt} \\
& + \beta_{12} Decentralization_{jt} + \beta_{13} X_{jt} + \lambda_t + \gamma_i + \varepsilon_{ijt},
\end{aligned}
$$

where FDI_{ijt} denotes real bilateral FDI stock of source country i into host country j in period t. $Decentralization_{jt}$ denotes the devolution of powers to lower levels of government in the host country. X_{jt} includes other characteristics of the host country which will be discussed further below.

The knowledge-capital framework of Markusen and Maskus (2002) suggests using six types of variables to explain the incentives for horizontal and vertical fragmentation of production at the bilateral level:

- the sum and squared difference between the source and host country economic size: $\sum GDP$, $(\Delta GDP)^2$;

[6]The list of source countries is as follows: Iceland, Japan, Switzerland, Turkey and EU-27 countries (excluding Belgium, Hungary, Malta, and Romania).

[7]The 19 OECD countries are Australia, Austria, Belgium, Canada, Denmark, Finland, France, Germany, Ireland, Italy, Netherlands, New Zealand, Norway, Portugal, Spain, Sweden, Switzerland, United Kingdom, United States of America. The main explanatory variable, the degree of tax revenue decentralization, is available only for selected members of the OECD which restricts the number of host countries in the analysis.

- relative factor endowments[8]: $\Delta Skill$
- three interaction terms of economic size with factor endowments which relate to the different modes of production fragmentation: i) $INT1_t$ captures vertical fragmentation and is equal to $\Delta Skill * \Delta GDP$, if $\Delta Skill > 0$, 0 otherwise; ii) $INT2_t$ captures horizontal motives and is equal to $\Delta Skill * \sum GDP$, if $\Delta Skill > 0$, 0 otherwise; and iii) $INT3_t$ also captures horizontal fragmentation and is equal to $-\Delta Skill * \sum GDP$, if $\Delta Skill < 0$, 0 otherwise;
- distance as a measure of proximity: $Dist_{ij}$;
- trade costs in the source and host country measured by i) tariffs as barriers $Tariff f_{it}$ and $Tariff f_{jt}$, and ii) bilateral trade costs $TradeCosts_{ijt}$ which include sharing the same language (*Common Language*$_{ij}$), and belonging to the same customs union (*Customs Union*$_{ijt}$), free trade agreement (*Free Trade Agreement*$_{ijt}$) or service agreement (*Service Agreement*$_{ijt}$)[9];
- and investment frictions in the host country measured by the ratio of the costs of setting up a business to outcome per capita: $INVC_{jt}$.

Carr et al. (2001) and Markusen and Maskus (2002) discuss explicitly the expected signs for each of these variables based on their theoretical model.

Furthermore, empirical evidence identifies a direct relationship between governance institutions and foreign direct investment decisions[10], while the literature on decentralization points out a potential interaction between the level

[8]Although GDP per capita is not a perfect measure of skilled labor abundance, I employ it as its proxy, since data are available for all countries and years under consideration. Furthermore, the empirical literature shows that there is practically no difference in the results whether GDP per capita or other factor measures are used (for instance, Egger and Pfaffermayr 2004, Blonigen et al. 2003).

[9]Each binary variable is equal to 1 when the source and host countries share the same language, belong to the same customs union, free trade agreement or service agreement, respectively, and 0 otherwise.

[10]Most of the literature has focused on the impact of corruption and property rights protection. Wei (2000) finds a negative impact of corruption on FDI flows and Mauro (1995) shows that corruption deteriorates economic growth through the investment chan-

of decentralization and the quality of governance (Enikolopov and Zhuravskaya 2007, Stegarescu 2005, and Kessing et al. 2006, 2007). Thus, to account for the impact of institutions I include a large set of institutional variables $Governance_{jt}$ - voice and accountability, political stability, government effectiveness, rule of law and control of corruption - drawn from Kaufmann et al. (2008), and the property rights index of the Heritage Foundation. Accountability and political stability are indicators of the political process and civil rights; government effectiveness is related to the bureaucracy quality; while rule of law and control of corruption consider aspects related to the respect for the institutions that resolve conflicts and govern interactions between citizens/firms and the government. A higher value of these variables is associated with better governance quality. Property rights protection ranges from 0 to 100 with again a higher value indicating better protection.

X_{jt} includes further characteristics of the host country, such as population from the World Development Indicators (WDI) and geographic area from the Centre d'Etudes Prospectives et d'Informations Internationales (CEPII), where I assume potential non-linear effects of country size on the FDI stock and add to the levels of population and area their inverse and squared correspondents (following Kessing et al. 2007).

Additionally, I include fixed time effects λ_t to control for omitted, time-variant effects that affect all country-pairs in the same way; c denotes the intercept term. In order to capture differences in reporting methodologies across source countries and other characteristics of the latter, I include source country dummies, γ_i. Host country dummies do not enter the regression equation as doing so I would eliminate the possibility of estimating the effects of decentralization, since the measure of administrative decentralization - government tiers - does not vary over time.

All variables and data sources are detailed in Table 3.10 in the Appendix.

Finally, I should discuss two methodological issues. Firstly, some of the explanatory variables are time-constant and the principal measure of decentral-

---

nel. Daude and Stein (2007) use a large set of institutional variables and show that Kaufmann's indicators influence FDI positively.

ization may be sensitive to business cycle fluctuations due to differing elasticities of the tax base of central government and constituent units even though the assignment of competencies remains unchanged. To solve the problem of a spurious relation between decentralization and foreign direct investment, I follow Stegarescu's (2005) recommendation of using period-averages. Thus, I create three-year-averages over the period 1994-2002 for all variables in the data set which dwindles the time dimension to three periods in total. Secondly, in my data sample there are a number of zero FDI observations which should be treated differently from positive values. A standard procedure in the FDI literature is to treat all zero observations as resulting from a censored process in which case the appropriate econometric model is Tobit estimation. Therefore, I use the maximum-likelihood procedure to analyze the effect of decentralization on multinational activities in the knowledge-capital model.

3.5 Empirical results

First, I present the results from the baseline model by considering different measures of decentralization. Next, I run a number of robustness checks. And last but not least, I address the potential problem of endogenous decentralization.

3.5.1 Baseline results

In the baseline specification bilateral FDI stocks are regressed on different forms of decentralization by the use of Tobit. In columns (1)-(3) of Table 3.2 I report the effects of tax autonomy and government tiers, included individually or jointly, on FDI. Columns (4) and (5) account for potential non-linearity in the degree of fiscal decentralization. Column (6) considers tax autonomy and tiers normalized by population size. Since Tobit coefficients are not directly interpretable, I calculate the marginal effects of the decentralization measures and present them below the estimated coefficients and their standard errors. The marginal effects are evaluated at the sample means of the covariates which may become problematic in the presence of non-linearity in the model (in particular, non-linearity in the degree of decentralization). Therefore, in Table 3.3 I list the results of the baseline specification estimated by ordinary least squares (OLS). The coefficients of all decentralization measures are identical in sign and statistical significance with those for the Tobit estimation and very similar in magnitude as well. The reported standard errors are heteroskedasticity-robust clustered by country-pairs along all specifications.

Overall, the baseline results provide consistent support for the main hypotheses, according to which a higher degree of decentralization decreases FDI and the effect of fiscal decentralization takes a U-form. The coefficients for fiscal and administrative vertical decentralization are statistically significant at least at 10% level and enter with the expected signs. First, the estimates of tax autonomy and government tiers in columns (1)-(3) and (6) are highly significant and negative. To make predictions about the quantitative size of the effects I refer to the marginal effects of -1.486 and -89.806 for tax autonomy and tiers, respectively, in column (3). Those suggest that a one-percentage-point increase in tax decentralization of the host country will diminish its inward FDI position by nearly 1.5 Mio. US dollars, while adding one more tier to its government architecture will decrease FDI by even 90 Mio. US dollars, which verify the first hypothesis. Second, in order to account for a potential optimal level of vertical decentralization I consider in columns (4) and (5) a non-linear structure in decentralization by adding a squared term of tax decentralization to the regression equation[11].

[11]The squared term of tiers has been also added to the regression; however, it drops due to collinearity. Thus, the analysis accounts only for a potential non-linear function of fiscal decentralization.

Table 3.2: Baseline model

Dependent variable: $FDI\,stock_{ij}$						
Variables	**(1)**	**(2)**	**(3)**	**(4)**	**(5)**	**(6)**
Sum of GDP	437.7599***	443.6877***	430.3019***	428.9523***	426.3081***	422.4551***
	(89.47797)	(93.41134)	(90.82349)	(88.41603)	(89.93046)	(91.45673)
GDP difference squared	-17.76277***	-18.28***	-17.9374***	-17.9152***	-17.98786***	-17.98719***
	(4.288602)	(4.432609)	(4.331673)	(4.285255)	(4.311397)	(4.389297)
INT1	1.569251	2.074084*	1.869325*	1.501616	1.766655*	1.805021*
	(1.091038)	(1.132937)	(1.107986)	(1.038531)	(1.069621)	(1.08213)
INT2	-2.494559**	-2.447004**	-2.429963**	-2.391746**	-2.336593**	-2.387881**
	(1.008632)	(1.058368)	(1.026713)	(0.9598138)	(0.9931117)	(1.001425)
INT3	-0.5537576	-0.7054409**	-0.6573801*	-0.5596399	-0.6380005*	-0.6733909*
	(0.3545469)	(0.3413824)	(0.3501011)	(0.3489594)	(0.3479223)	(0.3523912)
Population	-10.60063***	-10.01517***	-10.33014***	-10.54247***	-10.48387***	-13.59966***
	(2.659418)	(2.620733)	(2.609466)	(2.638071)	(2.602524)	(3.066929)
Population_inverse	-556.8233***	-984.3859***	-988.4203***	-496.8167**	-850.8376***	4028.523***
	(204.1793)	(310.7141)	(308.1867)	(195.432)	(306.8403)	(1116.394)
Population_squared	0.0073779*	0.0060628	0.0074924*	0.00964**	0.0094334**	0.017964***
	(0.0039865)	(0.0038849)	(0.0038678)	(0.0041123)	(0.0039631)	(0.00539)
Area	-0.0056542	-0.0780089*	-0.0827645**	0.0608572**	-0.0186519	-0.054205
	(0.0281456)	(0.0415277)	(0.041638)	(0.0289486)	(0.0455699)	(0.0359285)
Area_inverse	-282.1271	-2549.285	-1923.529	-120.5212	-1478.991	-710.9727
	(1453.871)	(1675.22)	(1612.275)	(1431.867)	(1575.889)	(1631.279)
Area_squared	1.49E-06	7.65E-06	9.31E-06*	-6.56E-06*	1.90E-06	5.27E-06
	(3.55E-06)	(4.73E-06)	(4.87E-06)	(3.62E-06)	(5.29E-06)	(4.28E-06)
Distance	-0.0016646	0.0000397	-0.0014265	-0.0042821	-0.0034626	-0.00183
	(0.0073567)	(0.0084031)	(0.0084957)	(0.0071915)	(0.0083791)	(0.0083382)

Table 3.2 continued: Baseline model

Dependent variable: $FDIstock_{ij}$						
Variables	**(1)**	**(2)**	**(3)**	**(4)**	**(5)**	**(6)**
Common language	144.1242***	151.4888***	152.2172***	139.0027***	146.006***	148.4359***
	(48.97282)	(50.89816)	(50.5458)	(48.40317)	(49.69204)	(50.37452)
Free trade agreement	50.80268	20.32129	38.13558	28.21545	24.41079	36.92173
	(124.3527)	(151.9592)	(149.0155)	(118.8982)	(145.1475)	(148.057)
Service agreement	49.69682	75.28452**	56.87954*	72.09113**	70.5954**	63.33604**
	(32.00945)	(31.11224)	(29.80006)	(34.26461)	(31.48404)	(29.94828)
Customs union	7.859837	-0.306103	5.012732	-20.81113	-15.91635	-3.857529
	(119.1601)	(146.8017)	(144.9735)	(115.0095)	(141.9085)	(143.8919)
Tariff_host	-7.619817	6.43654	-7.089948	10.09818	5.496567	-6.197698
	(10.55995)	(9.480393)	(10.37256)	(10.05587)	(9.282577)	(9.441621)
Tariff_source	-12.28303	-14.8718	-11.43088	-10.23084	-10.61192	-9.769255
	(9.597379)	(9.087555)	(9.178207)	(9.258083)	(9.127641)	(8.74423)
Set up costs	120.8764	264.7344*	145.9444	133.1568	133.9958	134.0201
	(140.7862)	(139.5087)	(141.4861)	(139.2224)	(141.8615)	(141.5539)
Voice and accountability	100.9308	-132.5403*	-1.064272	92.00779	46.78281	-4.15884
	(75.61209)	(68.30571)	(66.47488)	(75.62565)	(72.39905)	(59.66389)
Political stability	-105.3863	-126.3872	-166.7185*	-125.0397*	-158.5059*	-140.5026*
	(71.46707)	(85.47343)	(90.01242)	(73.61469)	(89.11638)	(83.21023)
Government effectiveness	175.1465***	180.0213***	148.8973***	192.2957***	171.9557***	62.07724*
	(34.35957)	(37.82388)	(33.67883)	(35.18583)	(34.39837)	(35.96234)
Rule of law	-296.6704***	-178.6526***	-157.1479**	-389.2492***	-272.0272***	-9.936677
	(75.95272)	(68.03925)	(67.0926)	(82.81841)	(73.66057)	(73.49988)
Control of corruption	88.65006**	-20.60942	8.987631	113.3168***	44.09524	-18.471
	(41.41482)	(30.81057)	(33.65502)	(43.60373)	(36.57815)	(30.24731)

Table 3.2 continued: Baseline model

Dependent variable: $FDIstock_{ij}$						
Variables	**(1)**	**(2)**	**(3)**	**(4)**	**(5)**	**(6)**
Property rights protection	0.2937895	3.816396**	0.7915633	2.110274**	1.762101	1.867751
	(1.022263)	(1.632271)	(1.280662)	(1.011367)	(1.336307)	(1.462182)
Tax decentralization	-2.472022**		-2.432753**	-8.594435***	-7.135391***	
	(1.038575)		(1.052508)	(2.181847)	(2.061478)	
	-1.487588**		-1.485967**	-5.162741***	-4.351278***	
Tax decentralization squared				0.1430761***	0.1056732***	
				(0.0353084)	(0.0360488)	
				0.0859469***	0.0644412***	
Tiers		-171.3705***	-147.0263***		-106.2476**	
		(51.82859)	(45.34277)		(47.11785)	
		-104.5982***	-89.80618***		-64.79149***	
Tax decentralization over population						-2.23E+07***
						(7209485)
						-1.36E+07***
Tiers over population						-1.72E+09***
						(4.62E+08)
						-1.05E+09***
Observations	1030	982	982	1030	982	982
Uncensored obs.	860	825	825	860	825	825
Pseudo R-squared	0.082	0.082	0.083	0.083	0.084	0.084

Notes: i) *** - significant at 1% level, ** - significant at 5% level, * - significant at 10% level; ii) Robust standard errors in parantheses; iii) All estimations include year and source country dummies; iv) All columns present Tobit estimates; v) The marginal effect for each decentralization variable is reported below the standard error of the estimate.

Table 3.3: Baseline model: OLS estimation

Dependent variable: $FDIstock_{ij}$						
Variables	**(1)**	**(2)**	**(3)**	**(4)**	**(5)**	**(6)**
Tax decentralization	-2.452643**		-2.290061**	-7.789118***	-6.092826***	
	(1.128381)		(1.106025)	(2.239863)	(2.113038)	
Tax decentralization_squared				0.1247553***	0.0856862**	
				(0.0355959)	(0.0382014)	
Tiers		-161.384***	-139.2095***		-105.5663**	
		(54.56493)	(47.95125)		(51.50521)	
Tax decentralization over population						-2.08E+07***
						(7541774)
Tiers over population						-1.67E+09***
						(4.91E+08)
Observations	860	825	825	860	825	825
R-squared	0.600	0.605	0.609	0.604	0.611	0.613

Notes: i) *** - significant at 1% level, ** - significant at 5% level, * - significant at 10% level; ii) Robust standard errors in parantheses; iii) All estimations include year and source country dummies; iv) All columns present OLS estimates.

As predicted, I cannot identify an optimal level of fiscal decentralization, but a U-shape relationship between fiscal decentralization and FDI. For an illustration of the finding, I calculate the expression $-4.35 * TaxDec_i + 0.06 * TaxDec_i^2$ from column (5) for values of tax decentralization between 2.44% and 54 %, which is the degree of tax decentralization of the most centralized country in the sample, Ireland, and for Switzerland – the most decentralized country in the sample, respectively. The total effect of decentralization proves to be persistently negative, ranging between -10 (for Ireland) to -47 (for Switzerland and reaching the minimum of -73 (at around 34% tax decentralization). There are four countries in the sample which pass this threshold - United States of America, Canada, Switzerland, and Sweden (refer to Figure 3.1). Although the latter four discourage less investment as a result of their high level of decentralization than Denmark, for instance, the result clearly points at the relative advantage which more centralized states have in the worldwide competition for international capital flows.

After the discussion of the main results, I look briefly at the controls of the standard KC model and the performance of governance quality. The sum of partners' GDP affects investment positively, while the squared GDP difference enters with a negative sign along all specifications. This is in line with the KC model predictions of a U-shaped relationship between the FDI position and bilateral differences in country size. Considering the three interaction terms, which indicate whether the type of investment is a horizontal or a vertical production fragmentation, the benchmark model yields negative signs for the last two terms and a positive one for the first interaction term. This result points at horizontal fragmentation which should not be surprising, since, typically, capital transactions between countries, which are similar in relative factor endowments and are integrated in the same market (such as the OECD member states) - are driven mainly by horizontal fragmentation decisions. All four bilateral measures of trade barriers have the expected positive impact on FDI stock, but are not always statistically significant. Furthermore, the host and source-country specific tariffs and the bilateral distance between the partner countries do not appear to have explanatory power for FDI. Surprisingly, the investment costs associated with setting-up a business, if significant, enter with a positive sign which contradicts the theoretical predictions[12]. Among the institutional variables, government effectiveness plays the most important role for FDI. This variable enters always with the positive sign as expected. I fail in identifying a robust impact for voice and accountability, political stability, rule of law and corruption, which may be a result of the high correlation of the governance variables among each other. Importantly, the estimate for property rights protection is always positive and very often statistically significant.

The main message of Table 3.2 is that fiscal as well as administrative decentralization prove to have a strong and significant impact on the investment activity of multinationals which is distinct from, and additional, to the effect of governance quality and the common KC controls. The OLS results in Table 3.3 give identical insights into the role of decentralization on FDI.

3.5.2 Sensitivity analysis

I begin the robustness analysis by considering alternative measures of decentralization in Table 3.4. Expenditure decentralization, though being an imperfect proxy for decentralization, in general, seems to play a negative role on FDI decisions with a significant coefficient of -2.309 (refer to column 1). Although it is reasonable to use more than one indicator at a time in order to catch different aspects of fiscal decentralization, columns (2)-(4) clearly show that expenditure decentralization and tax decentralization cannot be included jointly in the estimation due to the high correlation between them (larger than 0.70). To consider their joint effect without facing the problem of multicollinearity, I include a factor variable, containing equal shares of tax and expenditure decentralization, into the econometric analysis. Columns (5)-(7) show that the newly created variable performs equally well as tax decentralization, since it enters the regression with the expected sign. However, the magnitude of its effect cannot be interpreted, because it is not a share but a normally distributed variable with mean 0 and variance close to 1. The negative sign in front of the Tiers measure

[12]This outcome may be the result of the positive correlation between investment costs and government tiers.

remains negative and highly significant throughout all of the specifications estimated. To summarize, Table 3.4 reveals that alternative measures of vertical decentralization have a negative impact on FDI as well. Moreover, there is some evidence of the existence of non-linear relationship between fiscal decentralization and FDI. In the robustness analysis to follow I'll report regression results including government tiers, tax decentralization and the factor variable.

One can argue that the results for the different measures of decentralization have been influenced by the governance quality variables through the potential interaction between institutions and government decentralization. To account for that, I exclude Kaufmann's (2008) variables and the index of property rights protection. It becomes obvious from Table 3.5 that although the coefficients for fiscal and administrative decentralization change slightly in size, their negative signs and explanatory power persist in this specification. This provides me with evidence about the strong impact of decentralization on FDI irrespective of the inclusion of institutional measures. Government tiers prove to have here a lower quantitative impact on FDI than in the baseline model (compare the coefficient of -82.08 in column 2 with its counterpart in Table 3.2, which is -171.37). Due to the high correlation between tiers and institutional quality (ranging between -0.27 to -0.75), Tiers may have antagonized the positive effect of some of the governance quality variables and boosted their impact in the baseline model. Considering the potential non-linear effect of fiscal decentralization, the squared terms of tax decentralization and the factor variable enter the regression with the expected positive signs, but tax autonomy loses its explanatory power in contrast to the factor variable whose effect proves to be quite persistent. The latter finding may point at the relative strength of expenditure decentralization (as part of the factor variable) in this specification.

It is a relevant question to check whether the results reported above are dependent on countries in the sample with extreme values of tax decentralization. There are different forces behind an increase in the share of subnational tax revenues relative to the general government. On the one hand, once state or local jurisdictions receive some partial autonomy over certain tax rates or/and bases, like company profits or property, they will charge them and thus increase sub-national revenues. However, if the federal level still keeps power over the same tax bases, this vertical overlap will result in over-taxation. On the other hand, whenever subnational governments have full tax raising autonomy, they may decrease their tax rates which will attract a larger tax base. Eventually, horizontal competition will result in higher subnational revenues as well[13]. The same reasoning will be valid for other measures of fiscal federalism. To make sure that I account only for the vertical externalities associated with fiscal decentralization, I exclude the countries, whose powers are separated and distributed according to policy areas and in terms of fiscal decentralization they have competing and separate tax-raising powers and variable tax fees. These are also the countries with the highest degree of tax decentralization in the sample, namely Canada, Switzerland and USA. It becomes obvious from Table 3.6 that the negative effects of administrative and fiscal decentralization (the last being measured by tax autonomy and the factor variable) persist. More importantly, the coefficient of tax decentralization doubles in size and increases in statistical significance in comparison to the baseline results in Table 3.2. A major difference is that the squared term of tax decentralization which accounts for the potential non-linear impact of fiscal decentralization on FDI loses its explanatory power substantially. This outcome verifies the hypothesis of the general deteriorating effect of vertical decentralization. Moreover, it suggests that a U-shaped relationship between decentralization and FDI may depend on the sample and the inclusion of countries like Canada, Switzerland and USA, which are well known for the horizontal competition between their sub-national jurisdictions and, more importantly, clear separation of powers between the central, regional and local government tiers[14].

Vertical fiscal externalities usually emerge as a result of different government tiers levying taxes on the same tax base. In this context, it is interesting to test whether the effect of fiscal decentralization, in particular, persists with the inclusion of corporate income tax. While statutory tax rates are the

[13]I disregard the potential 'race to the bottom' for the tax rates which may result in deteriorating public finance positions for the subnational levels.

[14]Berkowitz and Li (2000) find out that investment tends to be higher in economies where tax rights are more clearly defined.

most available measure of corporate income taxation, they can be misleading since low statutory rates can be offset by a broader definition of taxable income (Benassy-Quere et al. 2005). According to Devreux et al. (2002), discrete location decisions by firms should be influenced by the statutory and the average effective tax rate, while the decision to increase existing capital in one country should be influenced by the marginal effective tax rate. Since the Tobit model accounts for the latter, I include the effective marginal corporate tax rate of the host country calculated by Devereux et al. (2002) as an additional covariate into the analysis. The results are reported in Table 3.7. The variable enters the regression with the expected negative sign. More importantly, the effects of both fiscal and administrative decentralization remain statistically significant and negative. However, this specification cannot verify the second main hypothesis - the existence of a U-shaped relationship between fiscal decentralization and FDI - which has been the case in the previous robustness check as well.

In a next step, I check the robustness of the dependent variable, the bilateral FDI stock, by replacing it with the bilateral FDI flow. These two variables together with the real affiliate sales are the most commonly used FDI measures in the literature. Thus, in order to enhance comparability between my results and those elsewhere, it is useful to reestimate the model with FDI flows on the left-hand side of the regression equation. The data are collected again from the EUROSTAT database. In Table 3.8, regressing the FDI flow on the standard KC model controls and decentralization yields similar results to the baseline specification. Although the number of observations slightly decreases, the measure for tax autonomy as well as the factor variable perform equally well as in Tables 3.2 and 3.4 with the only difference being the decrease in the magnitude of their coefficients (compare, for instance, -0.49 in column 1 with its counterpart of -2.47 in Table 3.2). Administrative decentralization represented by the number of government tiers also keeps its negative, though at lower significance levels, effect on FDI.

Table 3.4: Alternative measures of decentralization

Dependent variable: $FDIstock_{ij}$							
Variables	(1)	(2)	(3)	(4)	(5)	(6)	(7)
Tax decentralization		-2.204067*	-1.482383	-9.975987***			
		(1.22166)	(1.121876)	(2.559815)			
Tax decentralization_squared				0.1342262***			
				(0.0390069)			
Expenditure Decentralization	-2.309509**	-0.599337	-1.788628	-19.87941**			
	(1.12058)	(1.27581)	(1.335609)	(8.195616)			
Expenditure decentralization_squared				0.3297105**			
				(0.1419059)			
Factor					-48.8023**	-51.75008**	-67.20237***
					(19.83728)	(21.00802)	(21.77979)
Factor_squared							79.94149***
							(22.9494)
Tiers			-165.7456***	-131.0383**		-165.7364***	-121.0278**
			(50.25534)	(52.99625)		(50.00563)	(50.15416)
Observations	1030	1030	982	982	1030	982	982
Uncensored obs.	860	860	825	825	860	825	825
Pseudo R-squared	0.081	0.082	0.083	0.085	0.082	0.083	0.084

Notes: i) *** - significant at 1% level, ** - significant at 5% level, * - significant at 10% level; ii) Robust standard errors in parantheses; iii) All estimations include year and source country dummies; iv) All columns present Tobit estimates.

Table 3.5: Excluding governance quality

Dependent variable: $FDI stock_{ij}$							
Variables	**(1)**	**(2)**	**(3)**	**(4)**	**(5)**	**(6)**	**(7)**
Tax decentralization	-1.69401**		-2.427468**	-4.06431**			
	(0.8166157)		(0.95681)	(1.75954)			
Tax decentralization_squared				0.0367632			
				(0.0320307)			
Factor					-36.7711***	-63.28395***	-81.34154***
					(14.07283)	(19.28584)	(19.83886)
Factor_squared							70.29002***
							(20.45107)
Tiers		-82.08159**	-91.00499**	-84.0493*		-106.488**	-90.14691**
		(41.6466)	(42.87386)	(43.86922)		(45.46012)	(45.48184)
Observations	1030	982	982	982	1030	982	982
Uncensored obs.	860	825	825	825	860	825	825
Pseudo R-squared	0.078	0.078	0.080	0.080	0.078	0.080	0.081

Notes: i) *** - significant at 1% level, ** - significant at 5% level, * - significant at 10% level; ii) Robust standard errors in parantheses; iii) All estimations include year and source country dummies; iv) All columns present Tobit estimates.

Table 3.6: Excluding Canada, Switzerland, and USA

Dependent variable: $FDIstock_{ij}$							
Variables	**(1)**	**(2)**	**(3)**	**(4)**	**(5)**	**(6)**	**(7)**
Tax decentralization	-4.143305***		-4.36675**	-6.154747***			
	(1.482144)		(1.794893)	(2.145305)			
Tax decentralization_squared				0.0505448			
				(0.0354769)			
Factor					-43.68786**	-63.45841**	-61.44361**
					(20.95353)	(29.78255)	(30.45185)
Factor_squared							25.47777
							(27.40647)
Tiers		-161.9699***	-131.6619***	-120.5986**		-166.2291***	-157.0982**
		(58.88406)	(50.47001)	(53.47312)		(59.7799)	(62.97507)
Observations	851	803	803	803	851	803	803
Uncensored obs.	701	666	666	666	701	666	666
Pseudo R-squared	0.07	0.071	0.071	0.072	0.069	0.071	0.071

Notes: i) *** - significant at 1% level, ** - significant at 5% level, * - significant at 10% level; ii) Robust standard errors in parantheses; iii) All estimations include year and source country dummies; iv) All columns present Tobit estimates.

Table 3.7: Corporate income tax

Dependent variable: $FDIstock_{ij}$							
Variables	**(1)**	**(2)**	**(3)**	**(4)**	**(5)**	**(6)**	**(7)**
Effective marginal corporate tax	-176.0782*	-246.2853**	-137.5198	-46.56662	-221.1985**	-180.6526	-121.3892
	(105.1685)	(124.9672)	(108.272)	(75.93395)	(110.3596)	(112.4563)	(87.17654)
Tax decentralization	-2.56115**		-1.967139*	-5.677974**			
	(1.040643)		(1.036255)	(2.490854)			
Tax decentralization_squared				0.0744655			
				(0.0476015)			
Factor					-35.78893*	-27.56329	-44.62044*
					(20.99113)	(21.98188)	(24.97547)
Factor_squared							41.47386
							(28.31027)
Tiers		-166.4802***	-148.7954***	-117.5034**		-164.0142***	-139.6702***
		(51.00011)	(46.00065)	(54.60911)		(49.86823)	(53.26027)
Observations	926	878	878	878	926	878	878
Uncensored obs.	789	754	754	754	789	754	754
Pseudo R-squared	0.084	0.084	0.085	0.085	0.083	0.085	0.085

Notes: i) *** - significant at 1% level, ** - significant at 5% level, * - significant at 10% level; ii) Robust standard errors in parantheses; iii) All estimations include year and source country dummies; iv) All columns present Tobit estimates.

Table 3.8: FDI flows as a dependent variable

Dependent variable: $FDIflow_{ij}$							
Variables	**(1)**	**(2)**	**(3)**	**(4)**	**(5)**	**(6)**	**(7)**
Tax decentralization	-0.4941625**		-0.5837309**	-1.912525***			
	(0.2289019)		(0.2634943)	(0.5996515)			
Tax decentralization_squared				0.0297398**			
				(0.0117685)			
Factor					-9.549389*	-10.78621**	-12.94055**
					(4.969148)	(5.30491)	(5.491506)
Factor_squared							11.20227*
							(6.298426)
Tiers		-30.14602**	-23.21387*	-11.53239		-27.50464**	-21.03977
		(14.18839)	(13.55196)	(15.03397)		(13.64057)	(14.4963)
Observations	919	876	876	876	919	876	876
Uncensored obs.	644	619	619	619	644	619	619
Pseudo R-squared	0.062	0.061	0.062	0.063	0.062	0.062	0.062

Notes: i) *** - significant at 1% level, ** - significant at 5% level, * - significant at 10% level; ii) Robust standard errors in parantheses; iii) All estimations include year and source country dummies; iv) All columns present Tobit estimates.

In this subsection I considered a number of alternative robustness checks about the impact of vertical decentralization on FDI. The results clearly support the first main hypothesis: The negative effect of both fiscal and administrative vertical decentralization seems to be persistent along all modifications to the baseline model. The second hypothesis about the potential U-shaped relationship between fiscal decentralization and FDI has been also partly validated but at lower significance levels.

3.5.3 Potential endogeneity

So far I have assumed the level of decentralization to be exogenous, and have considered the impact of the degree and form of vertical decentralization on the foreign investment stock. However, Arzaghi and Henderson (2005), Panizza (1999), Fisman and Gatti (2002), and Enikolopov and Zhuravskaya (2007) point out the potential endogeneity bias related with fiscal decentralization in the context of different economic activities. Furthermore, inspired by the spread of political separatism and the emergence of new countries, Alesina et al. (2000) explore economic integration as driving force behind political disintegration. In this spirit, Shah (2008) and Stegarescu (2006) argue that world market forces make nation states diffuse authority and regulation to local and regional bodies. I incorporate these arguments by allowing for tax decentralization itself to depend on international investment activities. However, the degree of administrative decentralization measured by the number of government tiers is assumed to be exogenous[15].

I tackle the plausible endogeneity problem of fiscal decentralization by using two different approaches. First, I include the lag of tax decentralization as an explanatory variable instead of its contemporaneous value. Furthermore, an average value of decentralization over a nine-year period preceding the starting year 1994 of my sample is considered as an instrument as well. Thus, fis-

[15]First, the variable is time-invariant and dates back to the mid-nineties which coincides with the beginning of the nine-year-period under consideration in this study. Second, arrangements of the administrative structure of government tend to be persistent. Thus, just a decade-long FDI activity is unlikely to cause a major reform in the number of government layers.

cal decentralization clearly leads FDI in time and precludes potential reverse causality. Second, the model is estimated with the instrumental Tobit procedure. In the choice of instruments I follow Enikolopov and Zhuravskaya (2007) by associating the level of fiscal decentralization with the strength of national government parties. The reasoning behind lies in Riker's (1964) theory that political centralization, as expressed by fractionalization and age of government parties, reinforces fiscal decentralization[16].

Overall, the estimation results with instruments support the findings of the baseline model: Vertical decentralization has significant negative effect on FDI and a slight U-shaped relationship between fiscal decentralization and FDI can be identified. Columns (1)-(6) of Table 3.9 present the results from the inclusion of lagged values as main explanatory variables. The estimated coefficients are very similar in size and significance to the benchmark results. In columns (7)-(9) I explore the validity of the main hypotheses by instrumenting the degree of tax decentralization with government fragmentation and the average age of the three main parties in the host country collected from the World Bank Political Institutions Database (Version 3). Three major results emerge from the IV estimation: i) tax decentralization as well as government tiers keep their significant negative effect on FDI; ii) there is no significant evidence of a U-form impact of fiscal decentralization; iii) the signs of coefficients are the same but their magnitudes increase slightly in comparison to the baseline model in Table 3.2; iv) the identification of endogeneity is sensitive to the set of instruments considered[17].

[16]Although in the long run these variables might be endogenous to the model, nine years is a short period enough to consider them exogenous (cfr. Enikolopov and Zhuravskaya 2007). Furthermore, the two covariates do not play any statistical role on the dependent variable, FDI, when included directly into the regression.

[17]Let me elaborate on the last statement. Different potential instruments, for instance, surface area (the literature on fiscal decentralization demonstrates that the size of the country is related to the degree of fiscal decentralization), the share of population living in urban areas (as suggested by Stegarescu 2006), ethnic fragmentation (cfr. Enikolopov and Zhuravskaya 2007), and legal origin (refer to Fisman and Gatti 2002) have been included to the instrumental estimation. And although the first stage has always identified them as valid instruments for tax decentralization, the Wald test on the second stage of the estimation often failed to reject the null of no endogeneity.

Table 3.9: Instrumental variables estimation

Dependent variable: $FDIstock_{ij}$									
Variables	**(1)**	**(2)**	**(3)**	**(4)**	**(5)**	**(6)**	**(7)**	**(8)**	**(9)**
Tax decentralization							-5.211672**	-3.840103*	-6.582875*
							(2.116616)	(1.985042)	(3.535828)
Tax decentralization_squared									0.1410196
									(0.0875992)
Tax decentralization (t-1)	-2.621765**	-2.52177**	-7.370187***						
	(1.060801)	(1.05674)	(2.201692)						
Tax decentralization_squared (t-1)			0.1046826***						
			(0.0379654)						
Tax decentralization (avg)				-2.67912**	-2.880835**	-10.29217***			
				(1.167132)	(1.207091)	(2.576123)			
Tax decentralization_squared (avg)						0.1489692***			
						(0.0411537)			
Tiers		-145.3746***	-96.50452**		-166.3706***	-107.8782**		133.7408***	-111.6545**
		(45.19386)	(48.41251)		(50.16958)	(49.35795)		(50.33723)	(47.4956)
Observations	1030	982	982	1030	982	982	1030	982	982
Uncensored obs.	860	825	825	860	825	825	860	825	825
Pseudo R-squared	0.082	0.083	0.084	0.082	0.083	0.084			
Wald test (Prob>Chi^2)							0.056	0.379	0.519

Notes: i) *** - significant at 1% level, ** - significant at 5% level, * - significant at 10% level; ii) Robust standard errors in parantheses; iii) All estimations include year and source country dummies; iv) Columns (1)-(6) present Tobit estimates; v) Columns (7)-(8) present maximum likelihood instrumental Tobit estimates; vi) Column (9) presents two-step instrumental Tobit estimates since in case of more than one endogenous regressor, the maximum likelihood procedure has difficulty to converge (Wooldridge 2002); vii) Columns (7)-(9) have the following variables as instruments for tax decentralization: government fragmentation and party age; viii) The Wald statistic in columns (7)-(9) tests the zero hypothesis of exogeneity of the instrumented regressor.

I am aware of the problem of finding good instruments for my measure of *fiscal* vertical decentralization and for the other institutions in the model. As pointed out by Acemoglu (2005) all available instrumental variables represent just groups of institutional measures and as such are not suitable for disentangling the effect of only one variable. Although this claim may well be valid also for my empirical exercise, I can here again observe the negative impact of vertical decentralization on foreign direct investment. This thus appears to be an extremely robust result throughout the whole study.

3.6 Concluding remarks

Countries around the world are considering shifting authority towards their local and (or) regional governments and away from the center. The World Bank and the United Nations have even designed decentralization programs for the developing world and are actively encouraging countries to decentralize government activities, because decentralization is considered a propeller of economic growth and political stability. Decentralization may be beneficial for certain economic activities. However, in the context of FDI, governments should be concerned about the degree of fiscal decentralization and the optimal number of tiers building the hierarchical architecture of government. The key findings of this study point at the strong impact of decentralization on FDI. Cast in the knowledge-capital model of Markusen and Maskus (2002) the analysis shows that inward FDI decreases as the number of government tiers in the host country increases. I also find a consistent negative impact on FDI for the degree of tax autonomy and expenditure decentralization. The results are robust for running sensitivity analysis and allowing for potential endogeneity of decentralization. Additionally, the effect of fiscal decentralization tends to assume a slight U-shaped form. The results suggest that one-percentage-point increase in tax decentralization of the host country will diminish its inward FDI position by 1.5 Mio. US dollar, while adding one more tier to its government architecture will decrease FDI by even 90 Mio. US dollars.

3.7 Appendix

Table 3.10: Data sources

Variables	Description
FDI	Real stock of foreign direct investment from the source to the host country. The nominal FDI stock in Mill. Euro/ECU (until 12/31/1998) from EUROSTAT Database has been used. I convert the variable into US dollar by employing year-average bilateral exchange rate of the ECU/EURO expressed in US dollars from the International Financial Statistics of IMF. The series is then deflated by the US gross domestic product deflator with base year 2000 from World Development Indicators (WDI).
$\Sigma GDP, \Lambda GDP$	Difference / Sum of gross domestic products between source and host country in US dollars with base year 2000; Source: World Development Indicators (WDI).
$\Lambda Skill$	Difference of gross domestic product per capita between source and host countries in US dollars; Source: WDI.
Tariff	Tariff rates based on unweighted averages for all goods in ad valorem rates, or applied rates, or MFN rates, for source and host country; Source: World Bank.
Distance	Distance in km between the capitals of the source and host country; Source: Centre d'Etudes Prospectives et d'Informations Internationales (CEPII).
Common Language	A binary variable equal to 1 when two source and host countries share the same language and 0 otherwise; Source: CEPII.
Customs Union	A binary variable equal to 1 if the source and host countries belong to the same customs union and 0 otherwise; Source: World Trade Organization (WTO), own compilation.
Free Trade Agreement	A binary variable equal to 1 if the source and host countries belong to the same free trade agreement and 0 otherwise; Source: WTO, own compilation.
Service Agreement	A binary variable equal to 1 if the source and host countries belong to the same service agreement and 0 otherwise; Source: WTO, own compilation.
Population	Number of citizens in the host country; Source: WDI.
Area	Surface area measured of the host country in Tsd. sq. meters; Source: CEPII.
Set up costs	Costs of starting business expressed as of host country's GDP per capita; Source: Djankov et al. (2002).
Voice and accountability	Rating of voice and accountability in host country with a range from -2.5 to 2.5; Source: Kaufmann et al. (2008).
Control of corruption	Rating of the control of corruption in host country with a range from -2.5 to 2.5; higher values indicate better control of corruption; Source: Kaufmann et al. (2008).

Government effectiveness	Rating of government effectiveness in host country with a range from -2.5 to 2.5; Source: Kaufmann et al. (2008).
Political stability	Rating of political stability in host country with a range from -2.5 to 2.5; Source: Kaufmann et al. (2008).
Rule of law	Rating of rule of law in host country with a range from -2.5 to 2.5; Source: Kaufmann et al. (2008).
Property rights protection	Rating of property rights protection in host country with a range from 0 to 100; higher values indicate better property rights protection; Source: Heritage Foundation.
Tax decentralization	Ratio of discretionary sub-national tax revenues to total government tax revenues with a range between 2 and 55; Source: Stegarescu (2005).
Expenditure decentralization	Ratio of sub-national government expenditures to total government expenditures with a range between 10 and 58; Source: World Bank Decentralization Database.
Factor (fiscal decentralization)	Normally distributed variable which has been built through factor analysis. It comprises equal shares of Tax and Expenditure decentralization.
Government tiers	A time-invariant discrete variable with values between 1 and 6 equal to the number of central and sub-central government levels; Source: Treisman (2002).
Corporate income tax rate	Effected marginal tax rate in percentage points, Source: Devreux et al. (2002).

Table 3.11: Correlation matrix

		(1)	(2)	(3)	(4)	(5)	(6)	(7)	(8)	(9)	(10)
(1)	**Voice and accountability**	1.0000									
(2)	**Political stability**	0.6204	1.0000								
(3)	**Government effectiveness**	0.6423	0.5464	1.0000							
(4)	**Rule of law**	0.7480	0.7612	0.8249	1.0000						
(5)	**Control of corruption**	0.6872	0.7438	0.7753	0.9101	1.0000					
(6)	**Property rights protection**	0.4108	0.4550	0.4308	0.6215	0.5237	1.0000				
(7)	**Tax decentralization**	0.2782	0.1133	0.2173	0.2321	0.3052	-0.1128	1.0000			
(8)	**Expenditure decentralization**	0.2109	0.1137	0.1971	0.2929	0.3301	0.1433	0.6845	1.0000		
(9)	**Government tiers**	-0.7033	-0.7537	-0.4432	-0.5740	-0.6288	-0.2726	-0.0813	0.0087	1.0000	
(10)	**Factor (fiscal decentralization)**	0.2671	0.1237	0.2259	0.2855	0.3459	0.0144	0.9205	0.9150	-0.0404	1.0000

Chapter 4

Nation brands and foreign direct investment

This chapter is joint work with Kai A. Konrad from Max-Planck-Institute for Tax Law and Public Finance, Ludwig Maximilians University Munich, Free University Berlin and Social Science Research Center Berlin.

4.1 The research question

The state-of-the-art theory for explaining the size and the direction of flows of foreign direct investment (FDI) considers trade openness and geography as 'fundamentals' of FDI flows, and more recently added production fragmentation as an explanatory factor. This theory is known as the knowledge capital model (KC model). It takes into consideration that knowledge-generating activities such as R&D, can be geographically separated from production, and that these activities are skilled-labor-intensive compared to the actual production (Carr et al. 2001). A large number of studies use this theory as a workhorse, and augment the standard framework by further economic variables.[1] FDI may,

[1]For instance, the study by Kessing et al. (2007) considers the role of federal governmental architecture. Kalamova (2008) examines the role of measures of fiscal vertical decentralization. Blonigen and Davies (2004) provide an empirical assessment of the impact of bilateral tax treaties on FDI. Daude and Stein (2007) use measures of institu-

however, be driven by intangible factors that are often disregarded in economic analysis. In this paper we consider the role of some of these factors. We focus on the strength of variables measuring country stereotypes or consumer perceptions.

To operationalize these intangibles, we use the *Anholt Nation Brands Index*. This index is available for a large number of countries. It captures mainly individuals' perceptions about other countries, such as their governance regimes, products, cultural status, attractiveness from a tourism perspective, perceptions about the population, and about economic and social conditions. We ask whether these perceptions, stereotypes, or the quality of the 'nation brand' generate incentives for FDI, in particular, if we control for the 'fundamentals' that are used for explaining FDI flows in standard international economics.

There are several strong reasons why intangibles may play a major role in investors' decisions. First, stereotypes about a country may be used as a heuristic or a source of information about the quality of a country as an investment location. If the stereotype is that workers of a certain country are punctual, reliable and trustworthy, or if it is that its public administration is supportive and efficient, the information value of these stereotypes may make it more likely for the country to be an attractive location for investment. Second, if purchasing decisions by consumers are based on stereotypes about the country of origin of a product, then FDI may be a means by which a firm can take advantage of existing stereotypes. For instance, if a country's consumers have negative stereotypes about products from abroad, FDI in this country may give the firm access to the market in a country.[2] Similarly, if the widespread stereotype about a country is that the products of this country are of high quality and reliability, then FDI in this country may be a means to benefit from this reputation. For these and possibly further reasons stereotypes about countries should be important for firms' investment decisions.

---

tional quality, while Stein and Daude (2007) study the role of time zones and Gao (2003) the role of business and social networks on the location of FDI.

[2]Samiee et al. (2005), for instance, find that consumers often have misperceptions about a product's true country of origin.

For a general index that measures and aggregates stereotypes, we use the 'nation brand'. The concept of the 'nation brand' has been developed by marketing research and the difficulties of this concept have been widely discussed. Fan (2006), for instance, considers the nation brand as an umbrella brand, which is tied to the products of the respective country. Empirically, the nation brand is strongly related to the considerations on the importance of 'country-of-origin' labels for products, the study of which has received considerable attention. Bilkey and Nes (1982) survey a large stock of evidence that documents 'country-of-origin' biases for both industrial and consumer products. They emphasize the role of 'country of origin' as an informational cue. Some studies report consumers' home bias, or low ranking for US products by European consumers. Product evaluations are also seemingly positively correlated with the economic development of the country of origin. The meta-analysis by Peterson and Jolibert (1995) concludes that the country-of-origin effect is 'somewhat generalizable'. Verlegh and Steenkamp (1999) offer a further meta-study in which they confirm that the country-of-origin effect is a 'substantial factor'. They conclude that there is a strong link between country-of-origin and perceived quality, and that cognitive, affective and normative aspects and their interaction play a role for country-of-origin effects. Li and Wyer (1994) discuss that the country origin of a product can be a relevant aspect for several reasons. Among them, they mention country origin as a product characteristic, as an attribute with signaling value and as a means of applying a heuristic for simplified decision-making. Klein (2002) summarizes the country-of-origin effect: consumers use the country of origin to assess product quality and to optimize their consumption choice.[3] Given the role the country of origin may

[3]Moreover, Maheswaran (1994) discusses the effects of the country of origin on product evaluations within the framework of stereotyping and Johansson et al. (1985) add to the debate by taking into consideration the effect of familiarity and knowledge about the product class. Hong and Wyer's (1989) findings are that the country of origin not only has a direct influence on product evaluations, but also appears to stimulate subjects to think more extensively about other product attribute information, augmenting the latter's effect. In their analysis on how to remove negative country images Tse and Lee (1993) investigate the effects of decomposing a country's image into component and assembly origins, as well as the effects of global branding and product experience. Samiee (1994),

play for purchase decisions, the size and direction of country-of-origin biases should be important for multinational investors when choosing the location of production, and everything else given, investors should choose as their location of production countries to which consumers show a positive country bias.

These considerations are the basis for why the stereotypes associated with countries or, more generally, nation brand value should have an effect on location choices for international direct investment. We would, therefore, expect that FDI in a particular host country is driven, at least partially, by these perceptions and stereotypes. Whether this hypothesis is empirically sustained is the research question addressed in this paper. To assess this question appropriately, it is important to distinguish between a country's image, or the perceptions and subjective beliefs about a country, and the facts and fundamentals that are seemingly directly relevant for FDI decisions. Perceptions and subjective beliefs may be formed by marketing campaigns[4], large-scale events which attract international media attention, such as the Olympic games or other sports world championships, prejudices and images that are deeply rooted in the history of countries, but also fundamentals, such as a country's governance quality, products, income level and human capital skills. If these perceptions and subjective beliefs are simply a function of 'fundamentals' that are directly important for FDI decisions, the nation brands index should lose its explanatory power once we control for the 'fundamental' variables. Our analysis shows that this is not the case: the nation brands index carries independent weight.

We use as a dependent variable the bilateral FDI flows from 30 source countries to 34 host countries, taken from the European Union Direct Investment Yearbook by EUROSTAT. As regressors, we employ the fundamental variables used in the KC approach, and the *Anholt Nation Brands Index* - as our measure of those intangible psychological factors. We find that the explanatory power of the nation brands index is statistically significant and quantitatively large and picks up independent weight in the multivariate estimation. The findings are ro-

for instance, rationalizes the buying decision processes within the context of country-of-origin influences and links country-level considerations to firm-level decision-making.

[4]For a prominent example, see e.g. the large campaign "Germany, Land of Ideas" that was initiated in Germany (http://www.land-of-ideas.org/).

bust with respect to a number of alternative specifications. We conclude that we cannot reject the hypothesis that the nation brands index, and the perceptions and stereotypes which it is based on, have independent explanatory power for FDI flows.

In what follows, we proceed with the description of the main hypothesis, the empirical approach and the data in Section 2. Section 3 presents the results of the baseline estimation and discusses a number of specifications and robustness checks. Section 4 concludes.

4.2 Research strategy and data

4.2.1 The hypothesis

In the theory of international economics, flows of FDI are typically explained by what could be called 'fundamentals'. Intangible assets such as perceptions or stereotypes about countries, typically, play no role in these theories, even though, as has been outlined in the introduction, perceptions or stereotypes may directly or indirectly influence investors' behavior. We ask whether it is only the sphere of these 'fundamentals' which affects the decisions of multinational firms to invest in certain countries, and which determines the success of a country in its competition for international capital flows, or whether soft factors such as country stereotypes or perceptions about relevant aspects of a possible investment location play an important independent role. Our main empirical hypothesis is as follows:

Conjecture 3 *Consumers' perceptions and stereotypes matter for decisions on FDI, and they even matter if one controls for the 'fundamentals' which standard international economics accounts for.*

Our empirical strategy, therefore, is to use an index that measures such perceptions and stereotypes as a possible explanatory variable when estimating FDI flows in the state-of-the-art FDI model in international economics. As a measure of these soft factors - perceptions and stereotypes - we use the *Anholt Nation Brands Index*. This index maps the answers of individuals on their perceptions along different dimensions into a single index number. Individuals are asked about their perceptions of other countries, which may be summarized as follows:

- the country's attractiveness from a tourism point of view,
- their perceptions and stereotypes about the products from that country,
- their perceptions as regards the government in this country,
- their personal willingness to work in this country and their perceptions about social and economic conditions in this country,
- stereotypes about people from the respective country as employees,
- perceptions about the country's achievements in terms of culture, history and sports.

Our hypothesis is rejected if the index does not exhibit a significant effect once controlling for the 'fundamentals' that are usually considered the explanatory factors of FDI. If we cannot reject the hypothesis, we can interpret this as evidence supporting the theory that soft factors carry an independent weight for whether a country is attractive as a host country for FDI. In particular, we expect - controlling for 'fundamentals' - an increase in a country's national image to have a positive effect on the amount of FDI that is attracted by this host country.

4.2.2 The knowledge-capital model

The standard FDI model we use here is a merger of the horizontal and vertical models of production fragmentation that have dominated the literature on FDI. The horizontal model traces back to the seminal work of Markusen (1984) where a multinational enterprise produces in multiple countries to minimize trade and firm-specific fixed costs. In Helpman's vertical model (1984) firms geographically fragment production by stages. Recently, these two models have been combined into the KC model developed by Markusen (2002). This approach assumes that: "i) services of knowledge-based and knowledge-generating activities, such as R&D, can be geographically separated from production and supplied at low cost; ii) these knowledge-intensive activities are skilled-labor-intensive relative to production; and iii) knowledge-based services have a joint-input characteristic, in that they can be utilized simultaneously by multiple production facilities" (Carr et al. 2001). The first two assumptions explain vertical fragmentation decisions, while the third one motivates horizontal investment. Thus, the theory predicts that horizontal multinationals dominate when countries have similar endowments and sizes. Furthermore, horizontal FDI is encouraged by higher trade costs and higher firm-level scale economies. In contrast, vertical FDI is greatest when countries have very different factor endowments. The combination of small size and skilled-labor abundance leads to vertical firms, which choose the skilled-labor-abundant country as their headquarters country while the location of a single-plant depends on market size.

Carr et al. (2001) demonstrate a primary empirical specification of the KC model, which has become the workhorse for analyzing international investment flows. Subsequently, the model has been widely debated and extended in Blonigen et al. (2003), Carr et al. (2003), Markusen and Maskus (2002) and Davies (2008), among others. The empirical framework of the KC model employs a number of measures describing economic conditions and geographic characteristics of the host country, the source country, and between them in order to explain the motivation behind FDI decisions and the choice of investment mode.

4.2.3 Empirical specification

To test our central hypothesis about the relevance of the perceptions and stereotypes (aggregated in the index) for FDI flows, our empirical analysis is based on the KC model described above, augmenting the set of explanatory variables by the nation brands index. Accordingly, the variable to be explained is the bilateral flows of FDI from 30 source countries to 34 host countries as reported from the source country side. The data come from the European Union Direct Investment Yearbook by EUROSTAT. We consider EU-27 countries, excluding Luxembourg and Malta, together with Croatia, Japan, Switzerland, Turkey and the United States as source countries. The set of host countries comprises 34 developed and less-developed economies[5]. For our research question, the EUROSTAT data set is superior to other data sets on FDI (such as the International Direct Investment Statistics Yearbook by OECD or the World Investment Report by United Nations). It is well suited to our empirical strategy of examining the pattern of international capital movements for several reasons: a) national data have been harmonized, which makes a cross-section comparison possible, b) missing and zero observations are distinguished, and c) the member states of the European Union and some OECD countries which do not belong to the EU report data on their inward and outward investment flows. Our measure of FDI flows is explained by the following variables:

$$\begin{aligned}\ln FDI_{ijt} &= \beta_1 \sum GDP_{(i,j)t} + \beta_2 \left(\Delta GDP_{(i,j)t}\right)^2 + \beta_3 \Delta Skill_{(i,j)t} \\ &\quad + \beta_4 \left(\Delta Skill_{(i,j)t}\right)^2 + \beta_5 (\Delta GDP_{(i,j)t} * \Delta Skill_{(i,j)t}) \\ &\quad + \beta_6 Dist_{ij} + \beta_7 TradeCosts_{ijt} + \beta_8 Tariff_{it} + \beta_9 Tariff_{jt} \\ &\quad + \beta_{10} (Tariff_{jt} * \left(\Delta Skill_{(i,j)t}\right)^2) + \beta_{11} INVC_{jt} \\ &\quad + \beta_{12} NBIndex_{jt} + \beta_{13} X_{jt} + \lambda_t + \gamma_i + c + \varepsilon_{ijt}.\end{aligned}$$

Here, i and j indicate the source and host country, respectively, and t stands for year. The left-hand side variable $\ln FDI_{ijt}$ represents the logarithm of bilateral FDI flow. $NBIndex_{jt}$ denotes host country's power and appeal of a nation's brand image, X_{jt} is a vector of host country-specific control variables (each of these is discussed further below).

In Table 4.5 in the Appendix we describe all variables and the sources we collect them from, but we also discuss them briefly here.

The KC framework suggests using six types of variables to explain the incentives for horizontal and vertical fragmentation of production at the bilateral

[5]The 34 countries are the OECD member states Australia, Belgium, Canada, Czech Republic, Denmark, France, Germany, Hungary, Ireland, Italy, Japan, Korea, Mexico, Netherlands, New Zealand, Norway, Poland, Portugal, Spain, Sweden, Switzerland, Turkey, United Kingdom, and United States of America together with the BRIC countries (Brazil, Russia, India, China), Argentina, Estonia, Indonesia, Malaysia, Singapore, and South Africa.

level. These are, first, the sum and squared difference between the source and host country economic size: $\sum GDP$, $(\Delta GDP)^2$, second, relative factor endowments[6]: $\Delta Skill, (\Delta Skill)^2$. Third, an interaction term of economic size with factor endowment: $\Delta Skill * \Delta GDP$. Fourth, a measure of proximity, where we use *Distance*. Fifth, trade costs in the source and host country which are measured by a whole set of variables: $Tariff_i$ and $Tariff_j$ that capture tariffs as barriers, the interaction term $Tariff_j * \left(\Delta Skill_{(i,j)}\right)^2$ which interacts tariffs with differences in human capital endowments, and bilateral trade costs. The latter account for international barriers which result from (not) sharing the same language or (not) belonging to the same customs union or free trade agreement for the source-host pair and are denoted as $TradeCosts_{ij}$ - *Common Language*$_{ij}$, *Customs Union*$_{ij}$, and *Free Trade Agreement*$_{ij}$.[7] Finally, the costs of setting up a business as a percentage of outcome per capita accounts for investment frictions in the host country via the variable $INVC_j$. We adopt the interpretation of the KC measures and the expectations about their effects on FDI from Carr et al. (2001)[8].

---

[6]Although GDP per capita is not a perfect measure of skilled labor abundance, we employ it as its proxy, since data are available for all countries and years under consideration. Furthermore, the empirical literature shows that there is practically no difference in the results whether GDP per capita or other factor measures are used (e.g. Blonigen et al. 2003).

[7]Each binary variable is equal to 1 when the source and host countries share the same language, belong to the same customs union or free trade agreement, respectively, and 0 otherwise.

[8]They predict a positive sign for the bilateral sum of gross domestic product (GDP) levels and a negative coefficient for the squared difference in GDP between parent and host country, since investment is constructed to have an inverted U-shaped relationship to differences in country size, with a maximum at zero difference. The third construct which is the difference between the skilled-labor level of the source country relative to that in the host country is expected to be positive, because firms will be headquartered in the skilled-labor-abundant country. The squared skill difference reproduces the non-monotonic relationship between skill differences and FDI as predicted by the theoretical KC model. The interaction term of economic size with factor endowment differences should have a negative sign according to Carr et al. (2001), since investment is likely to be highest when the country is small and skilled-labor-abundant. Source country tariff is a proxy for trade openness and should have a negative effect, whereas host country tariff is expected to have a positive impact, taking into account the potential trade-off

In addition to the variables used in the KC approach, we include a number of variables with characteristics of the host country, such as population from the World Development Indicators (WDI) and institutional measures, which we describe later. Furthermore, we include fixed time effects λ_t to control for omitted, time-variant effects that affect all country-pairs in the same way; c denotes the intercept term. In order to capture differences in reporting methodologies across source countries and other characteristics of the latter, we include source country dummies, γ_i.

The core explanatory variable of our analysis is *Anholt Nation Brands Index*. According to Anholt (2005) this variable "measures [particularly] the power and appeal of a country's brand image". On a quarterly basis, a panel of 25,000 people across more than 30 countries is polled on their perceptions of the character and personality of 35 countries, including their own one. The total *Nation Brands Index* for each country is compiled as an unweighted sum of six different sub-indices: Tourism, Exports, Governance, Investment and Immigration, Culture and Heritage, and People. Each of these six areas of national competence are characterized by three to five questions, for which the answers range between 1 and 7 with a higher value standing for a higher appeal. We compile the data for the last quarters of the years 2005 and 2006 and supplementary information about the *Nation Brands Index* through the direct support of Simon Anholt's web site (earthspeak.com, Anholt 2005), and two global research companies conducting the index, GfK Roper and Global Market Insite, Inc.

An overview of the values of the *Nation Brands Index* in the host countries are presented in Table 4.1. The *Nation Brands Index*, which is the total sum of the values along all six dimensions described above, ranges from 94.22 (Indonesia) as its lowest to 131.44 (United Kingdom) as its highest value in our sample. The index varies slightly over the two years and remains essentially constant for some of the countries in our sample. In the next step, in Figure 4.1,

between goods trade and investment abroad. The interaction term of the host-country specific trade costs is predicted to have a negative effect. High investment costs in the host country are expected to discourage investors and thus have a negative effect. The binary bilateral trade costs will have a positive impact similarly to the gravity model in international trade.

Table 4.1: The Nation Brands Index

host country	**2005**	**2006**
Argentina	104.0	105.0
Australia	125.0	125.4
Belgium	117.0	115.5
Brazil	106.3	109.3
Canada	127.3	127.8
China	108.7	106.0
Czech Republic	101.6	104.6
Denmark	121.7	121.5
Estonia	97.3	97.2
France	125.6	126.9
Germany	126.4	128.4
Hungary	106.6	104.5
India	103.3	102.3
Indonesia	95.9	94.2
Ireland	114.7	115.9
Italy	126.8	125.0
Japan	126.3	124.7
Korea	103.4	101.0
Malaysia	99.4	97.2
Mexico	103.2	102.4
Netherlands	123.0	123.4
New Zealand	118.5	118.6
Norway	121.8	121.0
Poland	101.0	104.0
Portugal	114.3	114.0
Russia	107.4	107.0
Singapore	105.7	103.5
South Africa	98.9	99.2
Spain	123.1	122.8
Sweden	126.6	125.3
Switzerland	127.4	126.2
Turkey	95.3	96.6
United Kingdom	128.8	131.4
United States of America	124.9	123.9

Notes: i) Data has been provided by Simon Anholt from www.earthspeak.com; ii) The reported values are from the fourth quarter of 2005 and 2006, respectively.

Figure 4.1: The Nation Brands Index and log of FDI to GDP

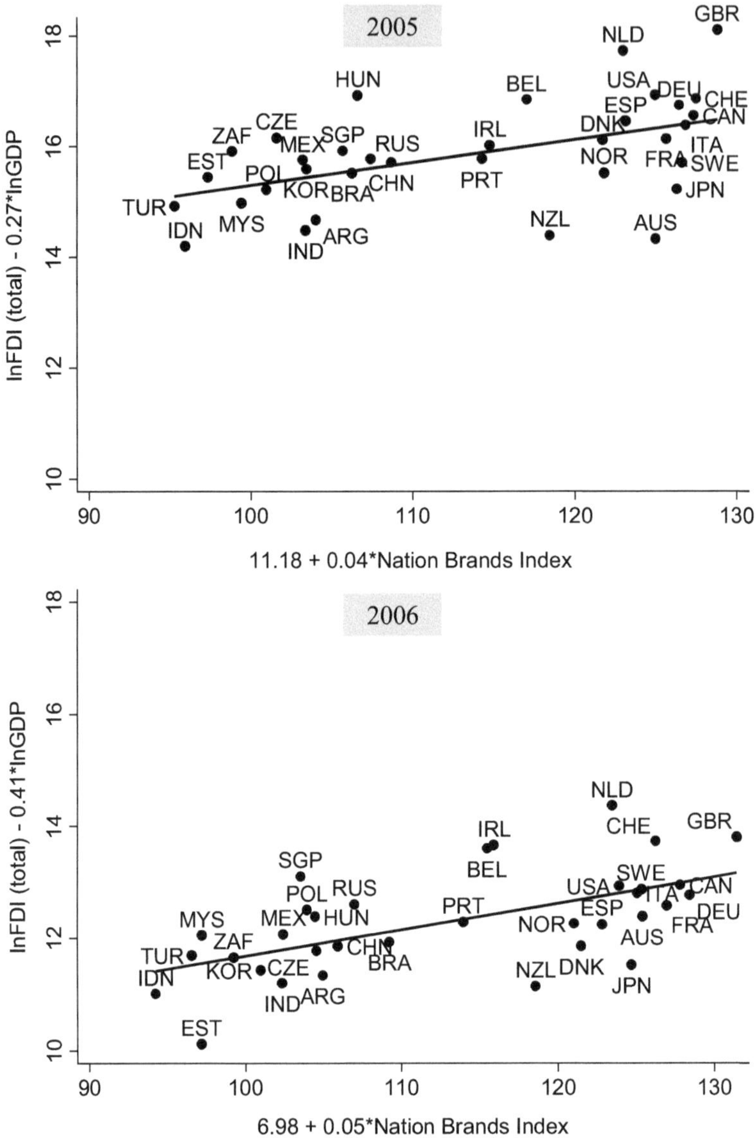

Notes: i) We regress $\ln FDI = const + \beta \ln GDP + \gamma NBIndex + \varepsilon$ for each year separately; ii) We plot the estimated $(\ln FDI - \beta \ln GDP)$ on the y-axis against $(const + \gamma NBIndex)$ on the x-axis.

we have a cursory look at the data by plotting the index against the log of total FDI flows into each host country relative to its gross domestic product for the two years under consideration[9]. The graphs foreshadow the results of a more formal analysis. *Anholt Nation Brands Index* of the host country appears to have a clear and seemingly strong positive impact on the incoming investment flows. Furthermore, a threshold value exists for the index at around 110 points which splits our sample into two groups: developed to the right and less-developed countries to the left of this value.

Before turning to the results of the multivariate analysis, we mention two methodological issues. Firstly, there are a number of zero FDI observations in our data sample. To address this we use a Tobit estimation which is a standard procedure in the FDI literature that treats all zero observations as resulting from a censored process. Secondly, some studies (among others, Blonigen and Davies 2004) find that due to the skewed nature of FDI data, the KC specification tends to yield non-normal residuals. This motivates the use of the logarithmic transformation of the left-hand side variable. It mitigates this problem in an analogous way to the gravity model in international trade.[10]

4.3 Empirical results

We first describe the results for the baseline model. Then we consider the robustness of the result by testing several modifications of the baseline model.

---

[9]For this purpose, we regress for each of the two years $lnFDI = const + \beta lnGDP + \gamma NBIndex + \varepsilon$ and plot the estimated $(lnFDI - \beta lnGDP)$ on the vertical axis against $(const + \gamma NBIndex)$ on the x-axis. Since a one-percentage increase in the GDP does not necessarily lead to the proportional increase in incoming total FDI, the estimated relationship above is to be preferred to the use of just *ln(FDI/GDP)*.

[10]Since it is important to contain the zero observations which provide information about why such low levels of FDI are observed, we express the dependent variable in our baseline model as $\ln(FDI_{ijt}+1)$. For high levels of FDI flows, $\ln(FDI_{ijt}+1) \simeq \ln(FDI_{ijt})$ and for $FDI_{ijt} = 0$, $\ln(FDI_{ijt}+1) = 0$.

4.3.1 The baseline model results

In the baseline specification we regress the (natural) logarithm of inbound FDI flows on the *Nation Brands Index* of the host countries controlling for all KC variables. The first column of Table 4.2 shows the results of the Tobit estimation. The Tobit coefficients are not directly interpretable, but we calculate the marginal effects by the McDonald and Moffitt (1980) procedure and list them in the second column. In addition, the third column reports the results for the baseline model estimated by ordinary least squares (OLS). The coefficient of the Nation Brands Index is highly significant and large, and the marginal effect for the Tobit estimation and for OLS is very similar. Despite the skewed nature of the dependent variable, many studies use the absolute value of FDI instead of its logarithmic value. To check our results against this part of the literature we report in columns (4) and (5) the Tobit coefficients and marginal effects, respectively, with the absolute value of FDI flows as the dependent variable. We report only heteroskedasticity-robust standard errors.

Summarizing, we find strong and consistent support for our main hypothesis, according to which host countries with a higher brand appeal and power face significantly higher incoming investment flows. The coefficients on the *Nation Brands Index* are positive and statistically significant at the 1% level and the numerical effect is large. In column (2) we report the marginal effects evaluated at the sample mean of the covariates. From this column it then becomes easy to calculate that a one-grade increase in *Nation Brands Index* is associated with a 27% (=100*[exp(0.238)-1]) increase in the flow of inward FDI. The Tobit specification yields a slightly larger estimate of the effect of the *Nation Brands Index* than does the linear specification in column (3), which is 21%[11]. Columns (4) and (5) reinforce the positive impact of *Nation Brands Index* on the incoming investment flows. However, the results are interpretable in a different way from those in the first three columns, since the dependent variable is in levels. The large *Nation Brands Index* marginal effect reported in column

[11]=100*[exp(0.1877)-1]

Table 4.2: Results

Dependent variable: FDI_{ij}					
Variables	**Tobit**		**OLS**	**Tobit**	
	Coefficients	*Marginal effects*		*Coefficients*	*Marginal effects*
	(1)	(2)	(3)	(4)	(5)
Sum of GDP	9.51E-13***	6.78E-13***	6.57E-13***	0.0008667***	0.0003255***
	(3.24E-13)	(0.000)	(2.16E-13)	(0.0001677)	(0.00006)
GDP difference squared	-2.16E-26	-1.54E-26	-1.5E-26	-2.30E-17	-8.64E-18
	(3.38E-26)	(0.000)	(2.27E-26)	(1.60E-17)	(0.000)
Skill difference	0.0003055***	0.0002177***	0.0001745***	61739.62***	23185.53***
	(0.0000567)	(0.00004)	(0.0000344)	(22838.54)	(7914.9)
Skill difference squared	3.08E-9*	2.19E-9*	1.19E-9	-0.1590386	-0.059725
	(1.77E-9)	(0.000)	(1.00E-9)	(0.4643258)	(0.17484)
*GDP difference**	6.82E-18	4.86E-18	1.87E-18	-8.79E-9**	-3.30E-9*
Skill difference	(9.17E-18)	(0.000)	(6.15E-18)	(4.32E-9)	(0.000)
Distance	-0.00074***	-0.0005274***	-0.0004118***	-244631.2***	-91868.14***
	(0.0001024)	(0.00007)	(0.0000566)	(55927.94)	(18089)
Population	9.34E-10	6.66E-10	5.51E-10	-0.8005587**	-0.3006397**
	(1.34E-9)	(0.000)	(7.93E-10)	(0.3816228)	(0.14503)
Common language	-0.753479	-0.5369666	-0.2518278	1.42E+9**	5.32E+8**
	(1.401568)	(0.99862)	(1.017244)	(6.49E+8)	(2.51E+8)
Free trade agreement	1.733162*	1.235137*	1.035571*	6.11E+8**	2.29E+8**
	(1.015232)	(0.72374)	(0.5779132)	(2.84E+8)	(1.04E+8)
Customs union	-2.145772*	-1.529184*	-1.140196	9.53E+7	3.58E+7
	(1.194345)	(0.85008)	(0.7004934)	(3.33E+8)	(1.25E+8)
Tariff_source	-0.6041231	-0.4305281	-0.1804822	-1.61E+8	-6.06E+7
	(0.5636157)	(0.40156)	(0.2195071)	(1.60E+8)	(5.88E+7)
Tariff_host	-0.2212904	-0.1577025	-0.1045936	501561.7	188355.1
	(0.1794374)	(0.1278)	(0.0864462)	(47300000)	(1.78E+7)
*Skill difference squared**	2.62E-10	1.86E-10	1.60E-10	0.1157189*	0.0434568*
Tariff_host	(2.42E-10)	(0.000)	(1.36E-10)	(0.0642253)	(0.02395)
Set up costs	-0.0284208	-0.0202541	-0.0110398	677503.1	254427.7
	(0.0188258)	(0.01341)	(0.0091944)	(5579758)	(2100087)
Nation Brands Index	0.3340842***	0.238085***	0.1876643***	94300000***	35400000***
	(0.0561223)	(0.03988)	(0.0318427)	(3.07E+7)	(1.04E+7)
Observations	1752	1752	1752	1752	1752
Uncensored obs.	1005	1005		1005	1005
(Pseudo) R-squared	0.09	0.09	0.40	0.01	0.01

Notes: i) *** - significant at 1% level, ** - significant at 5% level, * - significant at 10% level; ii) Robust standard errors in parantheses; iii) All estimations include year and source country dummies; iv) The explained variable in columns (1)-(3) is the log of FDI. The explained variable in columns (4)-(5) is FDI in levels; v) Columns (1)-(2) and (4)-(5) present Tobit estimates and marginal effects. Column (3) presents OLS results.

(5) means that only a one-point increase in *Nation Brands Index* suffices for an increase of inward FDI by 35 Mill.US Dollars.

We can also look briefly at the other controls in the baseline model. The sum of a host country's and a source country's GDP affects investment positively. The squared GDP difference enters with a negative sign (even though being insignificant) for all specifications. These qualitative results are in line with the KC model predictions of a U-shaped relationship between the FDI flow and bilateral differences in economic size. We find that FDI is strictly increasing in the skill difference. According to Davies (2008) this result should identify the predominant horizontal mode of production fragmentation among the countries in our sample. The interaction term between skill difference and difference in economic size in the country pair has an explanatory power at the 5% significance level only in columns (4) and (5). Its negative sign is in line with the predictions in Carr et al. (2001) that investment is most intensive when the country is small and skilled-labor-abundant. Distance has a consistent negative estimate across our results: a 100km-increase in distance is associated with a 5% reduction in the FDI according to our baseline specification in columns (1) and (2)[12]. Source and host country specific trade costs do not appear to play a major statistical role in contrast to the predictions of the KC model. Similarly, the three different proxies for bilateral trade costs - *Common Language*$_{ij}$, *Customs Union*$_{ij}$, and *Free Trade Agreement*$_{ij}$ - which according to the predictions of the theoretical model should have a positive sign, have weak explanatory power and the dummy variable for belonging to the same customs union yields a negative effect on FDI at 10% significance level. The negative sign, though insignificant, in front of the investment costs associated with setting up a business in the log FDI specification is in line with the theoretical predictions. In conclusion, many of the fundamentals of the KC model remain important determinants of FDI flows, but the *Nation Brands Index* is most powerful as a key explanatory variable.

[12]exp(-0.0005274)-1=-0.00053.

4.3.2 Robustness analysis

Let us now turn to some variations of the basic specification in order to check for the robustness of the basic findings. First, we account for the potential relationship between the quality of political institutions and the nation's brand quality measured by the index. There are intuitive reasons to assume this relationship. On the one side, the *Nation Brands Index* contains a "Governance" dimension, which builds up one-sixth of the index. On the other side, the way consumers perceive a certain country, as a whole, is heavily determined by the behavior of this country's government; thus, a strong national brand may be a direct consequence of good governance quality.[13] To account for that we add the following institutional variables - voice and accountability, political stability, government effectiveness, regulatory quality, rule of law, and corruption - drawn from Kaufmann et al. (2008). Accountability and political stability are indicators of the political process and civil rights; government effectiveness and regulatory quality are related to the bureaucracy quality and the existence of market-unfriendly regulations, respectively. Rule of law and control of corruption consider aspects related to the respect for the institutions that resolve conflicts and govern interactions between citizens/firms and the government. The values of these variables range between -2.5 and 2.5 with a higher positive value being associated with better governance quality. Because the six indices are highly correlated with each other, they will be included one by one into the model. It becomes obvious from Table 4.3 that the positive sign of the *Nation Brands Index* persists when we control for institutional quality. Furthermore, the magnitude of the variable remains the same and is still significant at the 1% level. In contrast, only two of Kaufmann's variables - voice and accountability and political stability - play a statistical role on FDI flows, however with the wrong, negative sign. These indicators seem to be correlated not only with

[13] Furthermore, empirical evidence identifies a direct relationship between governance institutions and FDI decisions. Most of the literature has focused on the impact of corruption and property rights protection. Wei (2000) finds a negative impact of corruption on FDI flows and Mauro (1995) shows than corruption deteriorates economic growth through the investment channel. Daude and Stein (2007) use a large set of institutional variables and show that Kaufmann's indicators influence FDI positively.

Anholt's index but also with GDP, since the statistical significance of our first regressor decreases with the inclusion of institutional measures.

There is a reason to suspect that the nation brand of a developed country affects its incoming FDI flows in a different way than that of a developing country. Moreover, from the graphical analysis of our data it becomes evident that the *Nation Brands Index* separates our sample into two sets, developed economies and less developed countries. Implicitly if not explicitly, the perception of consumers worldwide about the products, people, or government quality of a certain country may be a much more determining factor for a multinational company which plans to invest in a developing country in comparison to an investment in a developed one. To account for this we let the *Nation Brands Index* assume potentially different slopes for the two different groups of host countries. Specifically, we create an OECD dummy for all high-income host countries in our sample which are members of the OECD up to 1993[14], and we add an interactive term *NBIndex*OECD* to the list of regressors. The results are reported in column (1) of Table 4.4. As assumed, the effect of the *Nation Brands Index* on FDI decisions is slightly weaker when the host is an OECD country, since the interaction term enters with the negative sign. We run a similar empirical exercise by creating an EU dummy equal to 1 when both the source and host country in a certain pair belong to the European Union, and 0 otherwise, and using its interactive term, *NBIndex*EU*. The result in column (2) of Table 4.4 points at the fact that the nation brand will be of less relevance while investing within the EU area. This and the OECD outcome indirectly suggest the importance of *Anholt Nation Brands Index* as an information-bringer, in particular, about countries which do not belong to a well-known "league".

The availability of our main explanatory variable *Nation Brands Index* since the year 2005 restricts our analysis to the use of just two subsequent years. Substantial variations are unlikely to occur on both, regressors and dependent variable sides, for such a short period. It is possible that the significance of our

[14]The OECD dummy takes the value 1 when the host country is Australia, Belgium, Canada, Denmark, France, Germany, Ireland, Italy, Japan, Netherlands, New Zealand, Norway, Portugal, Spain, Sweden, Switzerland, United Kingdom, and United States of America, and 0 otherwise.

main explanatory variable results from the higher number of partially repeating observations. We can check and rule this out by running cross-section regressions for 2005 and 2006, separately. The *Nation Brands Index* keeps its positive sign and explanatory power at the 1% significance level in columns (3) and (4) of Table 4.4. In addition, another major KC regressor, $(\Delta GDP)^2$, appears statistically significant, which supports the idea that both the fundamentals in the KC model and the *Nation Brands Index* carry independent weights.

It is interesting to add further controls such as the effect of corporate income tax, market capitalization, and decentralization, among others. This does decrease the number of observations, but it does not change our main findings (we report the results in Table 4.6 in the Appendix). Also the exclusion of *Population* from the estimation does not change the results. Furthermore, we include Anholt's sub-index, which accounts for the "Investment and Immigration" dimension. The sub-index is significant and positive in sign when included separately. However, whenever we consider "Investment and Immigration" and total *Nation Brands Index* jointly, which are highly positively correlated with each other, the total *Nation Brands Index* emerges as the stronger one.

Our benchmark estimation does not address a possible reverse causality by which current inbound FDI may be a determinant of the *Anholt Nation Brands Index*. Almost as a *ceterum censeo* in empirical work, endogeneity is a possible problem. The actual FDI into a country may, in principle, have an impact on how foreigners perceive this country along the six dimensions captured in the *Anholt Nation Brands Index*. The use of FDI flows rather than stocks only moderates the problem if it is a problem. To further address this potential reverse causality we used the *Nation Brands Index* of the respective previous year rather than its contemporaneous value as our main explanatory variable in a robustness check. The results are reported in the last column of Table 4.4.[15] The results clearly validate our main findings: *Nation Brands Index* is statistically significant and has a large positive effect for inbound FDI flows.

---

[15]Due to lack of availability of more recent data on FDI flows, we can run this empirical exercise just for the cross-section of 2006.

Table 4.3: Governance Quality

Dependent variable: FDI_{ij}						
Variables	(1)	(2)	(3)	(4)	(5)	(6)
Sum of GDP	6.99E-13**	4.69E-13	8.5E-13**	8.9E-13***	7.7E-13**	9.34E-13**
	(3.47E-13)	(3.59E-13)	(3.63E-13)	(3.35E-13)	(3.58E-13)	(3.67E-13)
GDP difference squared	5.32E-27	-1.5E-26	-1.54E-26	-1.65E-26	-1.14E-26	-2.07E-26
	(3.58E-26)	(3.47E-26)	(3.55E-26)	(3.49E-26)	(3.51E-26)	(3.55E-26)
Skill difference	0.0002737***	0.0001874***	0.000282***	0.0002914***	0.0002604***	0.0003023***
	(0.000058)	(0.0000643)	(0.0000718)	(0.0000612)	(0.0000698)	(0.0000686)
Skill difference squared	3.23E-9*	3.26E-9*	3.0E-9*	2.96E-9*	2.89E-9	3.06E-9*
	(1.76E-09)	(1.76E-09)	(1.78E-09)	(1.78E-09)	(1.78E-09)	(1.78E-09)
*GDP difference**	5.84E-18	8.49E-18	6.74E-18	6.9E-18	7.18E-18	6.81E-18
Skill difference	(9.12E-18)	(9.11E-18)	(9.16E-18)	(9.15E-18)	(9.15E-18)	(9.18E-18)
Distance	-0.0007101***	-0.0005715***	-0.0007197***	-0.0007159***	-0.0007044***	-0.0007364***
	(0.0001022)	(0.0001083)	(0.0001085)	(0.0001094)	(0.0001059)	(0.0001105)
Population	-1.61E-9	1.64E-9	1.06E-9	9.21E-10	1.24E-9	9.44E-10
	(1.71E-09)	(1.35E-09)	(1.35E-09)	(1.34E-09)	(1.34E-09)	(1.33E-09)
Common language	-0.5654489	-0.5264229	-0.6752101	-0.6904277	-0.596557	-0.7420962
	(1.40064)	(1.398891)	(1.414133)	(1.411225)	(1.414689)	(1.413819)
Free trade agreement	2.342368**	1.994886**	1.724894*	1.765783*	1.630982	1.729467*
	(1.025106)	(1.012762)	(1.015045)	(1.018404)	(1.020425)	(1.014788)
Customs union	-0.8250611	-1.026482	-2.052456*	-1.909499	-1.96323	-2.131288*
	(1.271889)	(1.204902)	(1.209094)	(1.260788)	(1.200793)	(1.209121)
Tariff_source	-0.6329369	-0.6521663	-0.6051858	-0.6099395	-0.6100223	-0.6041819
	(0.5570095)	(0.5479186)	(0.5631937)	(0.5627296)	(0.5620749)	(0.5635761)
Tariff_host	-0.1571635	-0.4785349**	-0.2589841	-0.2765509	-0.3117021	-0.2278729
	(0.180435)	(0.1869047)	(0.1898789)	(0.19974)	(0.1947008)	(0.1926433)

Table 4.3 continued: Governance Quality

Dependent variable: FDI_{ij}						
Variables	(1)	(2)	(3)	(4)	(5)	(6)
*Skill difference squared**	2,24E-10	1.99E-10	2.68E-10	2.71E-10	2.77E-10	2.63E-10
Tariff_host	(2.41E-10)	(2.41E-10)	(2.42E-10)	(2.42E-10)	(2.43E-10)	(2.43E-10)
Set up costs	-0.0241429	-0.0807789***	-0.0337043	-0.033494	-0.0367608*	-0.0291225
	0.0186953)	(0.0224635)	(0.0211653)	(0.0206082)	(0.0200914)	(0.0205133)
Nation Brands Index	0.4023038***	0.3038007***	0.3330979***	0.3356156***	0.3412703***	0.3351621***
	(0.0603298)	(0.0563071)	(0.056294)	(0.0562059)	(0.0561469)	(0,0572582)
Voice and accountability	-2.183202***					
	(0.8358683)					
Political stability		-4.134126***				
		(0.9791213)				
Government effectiveness			-0.5217391			
			(0.9375797)			
Regulatory quality				-0.6249467		
				(1.057984)		
Rule of law					-1.024673	
					(0.8770034)	
Control of corruption						-0.0718911
						(0.8549284)
Observations	1752	1752	1752	1752	1752	1752
Uncensored obs.	1005	1005	1005	1005	1005	1005
(Pseudo) R-squared	0.09	0.09	0.09	0.09	0.09	0.09

Notes: i) *** - significant at 1% level, ** - significant at 5% level, * - significant at 10% level; ii) Robust standard errors in parantheses; iii) All estimations include year and source country dummies; iv) The explained variable is the log of FDI; v) Results are coefficients from Tobit regressions.

Table 4.4: OECD and EU countries; Years

Dependent variable: FDI_{ij}					
Variables	**NBIndex*OECD**	**NBIndex*EU**	**2005**	**2006**	**2006 with *NBIndex*$_{2005}$**
	(1)	(2)	(3)	(4)	(5)
Sum of GDP	7.15E-13**	9.23E-13***	2.14E-12***	2.43E-12***	2.44E-12***
	(3.41E-13)	(3.13E-13)	(4.09E-13)	(4.69E-13)	(4.71E-13)
GDP difference squared	-7.61E-28	-2.29E-26	-1.71E-25***	-1.17E-25***	-1.20E-25***
	(3.5E-26)	(3.31E-26)	(4.63E-26)	(4.1E-26)	(4.09E-26)
Skill difference	0.0002631***	0.0003427***	0.0004775***	0.0003555***	0.0003609***
	(0.0000576)	(0.00006)	(0.0000426)	(0.000039)	(0.0000397)
Skill difference squared	2.95E-9*	2.80E-9	2.07E-9	1.51E-9	1.53E-09
	(1.77E-9)	(1.75E-9)	(2.46E-9)	(2.75E-9)	(2.74E-09)
*GDP difference**	6.53E-18	7.04E-18	1.66E-17	-1.53E-17	-1.47E-17
Skill difference	(9.13E-18)	(9.04E-18)	(1.48E-17)	(1.19E-17)	(1.20E-17)
Distance	-0.0006949***	-0.0008147***	-0.0010953***	-0.0001863	-0.0002096
	(0.0001044)	(0.0001044)	(0.0001407)	(0.0001482)	(0.0001494)
Population	5.96E-10	6.44E-10	-8.86E-10	3.21E-11	-6.66E-10
	(1.34E-9)	(1.33E-9)	(1.93E-9)	(2.13E-9)	(2.12E-09)
Common language	-0.5853463	-0.9585952	-1,764627	3.573909*	3.587535*
	(1.391105)	(1.399717)	(2.19372)	(1.986033)	(1.982863)
Free trade agreement	1.569498	1.54673	1.957174	2.359017	2.260064
	(1.007707)	(1.008631)	(1.402693)	(1.479653)	(1.480655)
Customs union	-1.678915	0.4941939	-3.356886**	1.434405	1.524243
	(1.203228)	(1.546705)	(1.544214)	(1.6114)	(1.616213)
Tariff_source	-0.6016206	-0.6255232	-1.290379***	-1.390959*	-1.362247
	(0.5677785)	(0.5548401)	(0.4153521)	(0.8419687)	(0.841906)
Tariff_host	-0.3091071*	-0.2720795	-0.0200886	-0.926988***	-0.8807748***
	(0.1824458)	(0.18026)	(0.2292162)	(0.2921563)	(0.2954861)

Table 4.4 continued: OECD and EU countries; Years

Dependent variable: FDI_{ij}					
Variables	**NBIndex*OECD**	**NBIndex*EU**	**2005**	**2006**	**2006 with *NBIndex*$_{2005}$**
	(1)	(2)	(3)	(4)	(5)
*Skill difference squared**	2.63E-10	2.25E-10	-5.21E-11	9.2E-10**	9.10E-10**
Tariff_host	(2.41E-10)	(2.42E-10)	(3.12E-10)	(4.58E-10)	(4.57E-10)
Set up costs	-0.0104959	-0,0263637	-0.0469737*	-0.0286663	-0.0355359
	(0.0195105)	(0.0187993)	(0.0278548)	(0.0294519)	(0.0289979)
Nation Brands Index	0.5669078***	0.3857076***	0.4219751***	0.2907769***	
	(0.0988615)	(0.0603627)	(0.0702625)	(0.0678837)	
Nation Brands Index_(t-1)					0.2925871***
					(0.0688212)
*NBIndex*OECD*	-0.0521394***				
	(0.0184823)				
*NBIndex*EU*		-0.0321289**			
		(0.0125766)			
Observations	1752	1752	901	851	851
Uncensored obs.	1005	1005	508	497	497
(Pseudo) R-squared	0.09	0.09	0.07	0.06	0.06

Notes: i) *** - significant at 1% level, ** - significant at 5% level, * - significant at 10% level; ii) Robust standard errors in parantheses; iii) The estimations in columns (1)-(2) include year and source country dummies; iv) Columns (3)-(4) present cross-section estimation results; v) Column (5) reports the results of a cross-section regression for the year 2006 with the 2005 value of *NBIndex*; vi) The explained variable is the log of FDI; vii) Results are from Tobit regressions.

4.4 Concluding remarks

Governments invest (or investigate opportunities to invest) into an improvement of the country's image. The considerable competition for attracting major cultural events or sports championships, the international competition for the Olympic games, but also marketing campaigns such as *Germany, Land of Ideas* and the campaign for *Cool Britannia* are recent examples, and these may affect beliefs, stereotypes or prejudices about countries which are mapped in a nation's brand index. We show that a nation's brand index (as measured by *Anholt Nation Brands Index*) indeed has some independent effect for one of the key variables of a country's economic prosperity: inbound FDI. We show that FDI flows into a host country rise as its nation image, the value of its intangibles, improves. We also show that this effect is not driven by 'fundamental' or 'economic' variables that are known from international economics to influence FDI flows. For this purpose we use the theory-based KC model which includes the main economic variables and is the workhorse for explaining FDI in international economics. We show that a nation brands index bears considerable explanatory weight in this multivariate analysis. Our analysis provides strong evidence suggesting that intangibles - stereotypes and perceptions - indeed matter for investment decisions. We find that the *Anholt Nation Brands Index*, our measure for intangibles in the host country, has a large positive effect on FDI: a one-point increase in the index is associated with a 27% increase in the flow of inward FDI. Moreover, the index plays a role for both developing and developed countries with the effect being weaker for the latter group.

4.5 Appendix

Table 4.5: Data sources

Variables	Description
FDI	Flow of foreign direct investment from the source to the host country. We use the nominal FDI flow in Euro from EUROSTAT Database. We convert the variable into US dollars by employing year-average bilateral exchange rate of the EURO expressed in US dollars from the International Financial Statistics of IMF.
$\Sigma GDP, \Lambda GDP$	Difference / Sum of gross domestic products between source and host country in US dollars with base year 2000; Source: World Development Indicators (WDI).
$\Lambda Skill$	Difference of gross domestic product per capita between source and host countries in US dollars; Source: WDI.
Tariff	Tariff rates based on unweighted averages for all goods in ad valorem rates, or applied rates, or MFN rates, for source and host country; Source: World Bank.
Distance	Distance in km between the capitals of the source and host country; Source: Centre d'Etudes Prospectives et d'Informations Internationales (CEPII).
Common Language	A binary variable equal to 1 when two source and host countries share the same language and 0 otherwise; Source: CEPII.
Customs Union	A binary variable equal to 1 if the source and host countries belong to the same customs union and 0 otherwise; Source: World Trade Organization (WTO), own compilation.
Free Trade Agreement	A binary variable equal to 1 if the source and host countries belong to the same free trade agreement and 0 otherwise; Source: WTO, own compilation.
Population	Number of citizens in the host country; Source: WDI.
Set up costs	Costs of starting business expressed as of host country's GDP per capita; Source: Djankov et al. (2002).
Voice and accountability	Rating of voice and accountability in host country with a range from -2.5 to 2.5; Source: Kaufmann et al. (2008).
Control of corruption	Rating of the control of corruption in host country with a range from -2.5 to 2.5; higher values indicate better control of corruption; Source: Kaufmann et al. (2008).
Government effectiveness	Rating of government effectiveness in host country with a range from -2.5 to 2.5; Source: Kaufmann et al. (2008).
Regulatory quality	Rating of regulatory quality in host country with a range from -2.5 to 2.5; Source: Kaufmann et al. (2008).
Political stability	Rating of political stability in host country with a range from -2.5 to 2.5; Source: Kaufmann et al. (2008).
Rule of law	Rating of rule of law in host country with a range from -2.5 to 2.5; Source: Kaufmann et al. (2008).

Market capitalization	Average market capitalization as a percentage of GDP in host country calculated by dividing the value of traded stocks in percent of GDP through the turnover ratio; Source: WDI.
Government tiers	A time-invariant discrete variable with values between 1 and 6 equal to the number of central and sub-central government levels; Source: Treisman (2002).
Corporate income tax rate	Highest marginal tax rate measured in percentage points for the year 2004; Source: WDI.
Nation Brands Index	A measure of country's brand image ranging between the values of 95 and 132 in our sample; Source: Simon Anholt (earthspeak.com).

Table 4.6: Further robustness check

Dependent variable: FDI_{ij}						
Variables	(1)	(2)	(3)	(4)	(5)	(6)
Sum of GDP	1.06E-12***	8.37E-13**	1.00E-12***	1.03E-12***	1.40E-12***	1.04E-12***
	(3.19E-13)	(3.41E-13)	(3.30E-13)	(2.94E-13)	(3.15E-13)	(3.46E-13)
GDP difference squared	-3.08E-26	-1.55E-26	-3.00E-26	-2.36E-26	-7.54E-26**	-3.22E-26
	(3.38E-26)	(3.43E-26)	(3.54E-26)	(3.35E-26)	(3.3E-26)	(3.88E-26)
Skill difference	0.0003314***	0.0003142***	0.000309***	0.0003127***	0.0002957***	0.0003084***
	(0.0000576)	(0.000066)	(0.0000588)	(0.0000539)	(0.0000568)	(0.0000573)
Skill difference squared	3.31E-09*	2.44E-09	2.92E-09	3.15E-09*	3.09E-09*	3.11E-09*
	(1.77E-09)	(1.80E-09)	(1.84E-09)	(1.76E-09)	(1.77E-09)	(1.77E-09)
*GDP difference**	7.29E-18	8.66E-18	8.91E-18	5.39E-18	9.98E-18	7.44E-18
Skill difference	(9.22E-18)	(9.26E-18)	(9.83E-18)	(8.72E-18)	(9.23E-18)	(9.35E-18)
Distance	-0.0007537***	-0.0007478***	-0.0007551***	-0.0007523***	-0.0007808***	-0.0007501***
	(0.0001032)	(0.0001197)	(0.0001096)	(0.0000999)	(0.0001036)	(0.0001048)
Population	9.08E-10	1.06E-09	1.26E-09		1.98E-09	1.14E-09
	(1.33E-09)	(1.47E-09)	(3.25E-09)		(1.31E-09)	(1.43E-09)
Common language	-1.034106	-0.9553246	-0.7814387	-0.7545036	-1.070248	-0.8413477
	(1.412529)	(1.48174)	(1.42315)	(1.401607)	(1.416519)	(1.42005)
Free trade agreement	1.273871	1.306075	1.685297	1.669293*	1.704653*	1.73633*
	(1.051327)	(1.221236)	(1.027178)	(1.003698)	(1.014496)	(1.015299)
Customs union	-1.665566	-2.307559*	-2.250431*	-2.256678*	-2.182434*	-2.194358*
	(1.194665)	(1.269016)	(1.232345)	(1.168625)	(1.206132)	(1.202745)
Tariff_source	-0.5937343	-0.7184805	-0.6039676	-0.6044291	-0.5767961	-0.5971736
	(0.5586368)	(0.5720441)	(0.5718108)	(0.5634317)	(0.5616399)	(0.5631714)
Tariff_host	-0.1967495	-0.2742201	-0.2377854	-0.2041618	-0.1461294	-0.2055091
	(0.1786715)	(0.1848234)	(0.2002899)	(0.1786414)	(0.1802932)	(0.1815714)

Table 4.6 continued: Further robustness check

Dependent variable: FDI_{ij}						
Variables	(1)	(2)	(3)	(4)	(5)	(6)
*Skill difference squared**	1.88E-10	2.35E-10	2.90E-10	2.86E-10	2.41E-10	2.56E-10
Tariff_host	(2.42E-10)	(2.45E-10)	(2.56E-10)	(2.39E-10)	(2.43E-10)	(2.43E-10)
Set up costs	-0.0222154	-0.0289305	-0.0300443	-0.0275478	-0.0309931*	-0.028518
	(0.0189232)	(0.0236941)	(0.0217442)	(0.0188159)	(0.0186672)	(0.0187957)
Nation Brands Index	0.330244***	0.3380943***	0.3350051***	0.3383826***		0.2668841*
	(0.0555309)	(0.0709361)	(0.0567056)	(0.0550058)		(0.1473141)
NBIndex Investment					1.262109***	0.280376
					(0.2212142)	(0.5829575)
Market capitalization	0.0132408**					
	(0.0055382)					
Government tiers		0.1716182				
		(0.8572914)				
Corporate income tax rate			-0.016611			
			(0.049158)			
Observations	1752	1646	1699	1752	1752	1752
Uncensored obs.	1005	948	966	1005	1005	1005
(Pseudo) R-squared	0.09	0.08	0.08	0.09	0.09	0.09

Notes: i) *** - significant at 1% level, ** - significant at 5% level, * - significant at 10% level; ii) Robust standard errors in parantheses; iii) All estimations include year and source country dummies; iv) The explained variable is the log of FDI; v) Results are coefficients from Tobit regressions; vi) Market capitalization in column (1) is measured as a percentage of GDP of the host country; vii) In column (2) *Government tiers* is a proxy for the degree of decentralization in the host country; viii) In column (3) *Corporate income tax rate* measures the highest marginal corporate tax rate for each host country in year 2004.

Summary in German

Die hier vorgelegte Dissertation ist eine Sammlung von drei Essays im Bereich des internationalen Handels und der öffentlichen Finanzen. Alle drei beschäftigen sich mit dem Verhältnis zwischen Struktur und Qualität des öffentlichen Sektors sowie dem Prozess der wirtschaftlichen Integration. Des Weiteren werden in den Essays die Instrumente und Methoden der Panel-Data-Ökonometrie zur Untersuchung und Analyse angewandt. Kapitel 2 und 3 untersuchen die Auswirkungen der Regierungs- bzw. Staatstrukturen, insbesondere, das Ausmaß und die Form der Regierungsdezentralisierung, im Handel sowie im Bereich der Fremddirektinvestitionen. Kapitel 4 betrachtet zusätzlich die Rolle von den immateriellen Aktiva ("intangibles") des Staates im Zusammenhang mit Auslandsdirektinvestitionen.

Studien zum internationalen Handel. Die Literatur zum internationalen Handel untersucht die Unternehmensgegebenheiten und Marktbedingungen, die ein Unternehmen dazu bewegen, seine Produkte ins Ausland zu exportieren oder sie vor Ort über ausländische Direktinvestitionen herzustellen. Das etablierte empirische Modell bei der Analyse von bilateralen Handelsströmen ist die sogenannte Gravitäts-Gleichung. In der Standardversion dieser Gleichung werden bilaterale Handelsströme positiv von der ökonomischen Größe der Handelspartner und negativ von den Handelskosten und Entfernung zwischen ihnen beeinflusst. Die empirische Analyse zu bilateralen ausländischen Investitionen bedient sich alternative Allgemeingleichgewichtsmodelle. Das meistbekannte Modell ist das sogenannte "Knowledge-Capital"-Modell, das zwischen horizontalen und vertikalen Investitionsmotivationen differenzieren kann.

Studien zur Regierungsstruktur. Die Hauptfunktionen des öffentlichen Sektors beinhalten die effiziente Bereitstellung von öffentlichen Gütern, die Gewährleistung der sozialen Gleichheit durch Einkommensverteilung, und Sicherung der makroökonomischen und politischen Stabilität des Landes. Die richtige Ausführung dieser Aufgaben hängt von der Art und Weise, in der der Staat organisiert ist. Die Regierungsorganisationen vieler Staaten der Welt werden transformiert, indem Ressourcen und Entscheidungskompetenzen von der zentralen zu den lokalen und regionalen Regierungsebenen übertragen werden. Dieser Prozess wird Dezentralisierung genannt und ist der Hauptgegenstand der Analyse in der ökonomischen Literatur zur Struktur des Staates.

Handel und Dezentralisierung. Kapital 2 ist durch Zusammenarbeit mit Prof. Dr. Sebastian G. Kessing entstanden. Zunehmende Globalisierung von ökonomischen Aktivitäten und Dezentralisierung der Regierungsstrukturen wurden vielfältig betrachtet und diskutiert, aber normalerweise nicht miteinander in Verbindung gebracht. Einerseits hat die Literatur zum internationalen Handel ausgiebig die Bedingungen und Konsequenzen des internationalen Handels erforscht. Andererseits hat die Literatur zum fiskalen Föderalismus untersucht, wie Länder sich in Grad und Form unterscheiden, in welcher die Entscheidungsgewalten über verschiedene Ebenen der Regierung hinweg angesiedelt sind.

Kapitel 2 betont das Verhältnis zwischen der länderspezifischen Regierungsarchitektur und der ökonomischen Integration mit dem Rest der Welt. Insbesondere untersucht es empirisch wie Dezentralisierung den Auslands- und Binnenhandel beeinflusst. Diese Frage ist bedeutend sowohl für Wirtschaftswissenschaftler im Bereich des Handels und öffentlichen Finanzen, sowie für politische Entscheidungsträger, die sich einen Trend von Dezentralisierungsreformen gegenübersehen.

Die empirische Analyse dieses Kapitels basiert auf dem Standardgravitätsmodell und umfasst 39 Länder über eine Zeitspanne von 20 Jahren (1980-1999). Sie unterscheidet zwischen ausländischem und inländischem Handel und integriert die "multilateral resistance terms" von Anderson und van Wincoop (2003) über länderspezifische fixe Effekte. Diese Arbeit liefert eine bedeutende Erweiterung zu den bestehenden Standardspezifikationen des Gravitätsmodells, indem es erstens Import- und Exportlandsspezifische Messgrößen der Dezentralisierung berücksichtigt und zweitens eine Beziehung zwischen dem Grad der Dezentralisierung des Landes und dem sogenannten "home bias" aufzeigt. Letzteres bezeichnet die potenzielle Auswirkung der Dezentralisierung auf die Präferenz für inländischen Handel.

Die Haupterkenntnisse des zweiten Kapitels können wie folgt zusammengefasst werden: Dezentralisierung, gemessen an dem Grad der Ausgabendezentralisierung, spielt eine signifikante Rolle auf das Volumen von Handelsströmen. Einerseits tendiert sie dazu, den nationalen Handel zu reduzieren, andererseits fördert sie den bilateralen Handel. Der Grund fürs erste Ergebnis liegt in der Fragmentierung des Innenmarktes durch Dezentralisierung. Lokale Regierungen nutzen oft ihre Regulierungsmacht als Schutzmechanismus, um Barrieren zu erstellen, die interne Handelstransaktionen kostspieliger machen. Hingegen werden internationale Güter den verteuerten nationalen Gütern bevorzugt, was das zweite Ergebnis erklärt. Eine alternative Erklärung für die Beziehung zwischen Dezentralisierung und internationalem Handel kann in der Substitutionsbeziehung zwischen ausländischen Direktinvestitionen und ausländischem Handel gefunden werden.

Ebenso trägt diese Arbeit zu einem besseren Verständnis der Größe des "border effect" (oder "home bias") im internationalen Handel bei. Es wird aufgezeigt, dass Länder mit einer sehr hohen fiskalen Dezentralisierung ein zweimal so niedriges "home bias" im Vergleich zu stark zentralisierten Mitspielern aufweisen.

Ausländische Direktinvestitionen und Dezentralisierung. Kapitel 3 geht der Frage nach, ob Länder mit zentralisierter Regierungsstruktur einen Vorteil gegenüber den mehr dezentralisierten Gegenspielern im Wettbewerb um ausländische Direktinvestitionen haben. Im Einzelnen wird gefragt wie verschiedene Formen und Stufen der Dezentralisierung Fremddirektinvestitionen beeinflussen. Dies ist eine bedeutende Frage, weil die Entscheidung eines multinationalen Unternehmens, einen spezifischen ausländischen Markt durch Auslagerung der Produktion dort zu bedienen, größtenteils davon abhängt, wie die Regierungs- bzw. Staatsstrukturen das Investitionsklima an dem gewünschten Standort gestalten. Insbesondere haben die Regierungsstrukturen einen maßgeblichen Einfluss, wenn es sich um Besteuerung und Regulierung, Bereitstellung von Infrastruktur, und weitere Regierungserscheinungen wie Korruption handelt, die alle Bestimmungsfaktoren für ausländische Direktinvestitionen sind.

Die formale Analyse zum Zusammenhang zwischen Dezentralisierung und ausländischen Direktinvestitionen ist in dem empirischen "Knowledge-Capital"-Modell von Markusen und Maskus (2002) dargestellt. Es werden 28 Investorenländer (source countries), hauptsächlich europäische Mitgliedsstaaten, und 19 OECD Gastländer (host countries) über eine Periode von neun Jahren (1994-2002) betrachtet. Die Standardfaktoren des "Knowledge-Capital"-Modells werden durch verschiedene Dezentralisierungsvariablen ergänzt, um deren Einfluss auf die ausländischen Investitionen zu untersuchen. Die herausragende Stärke dieser empirischen Analyse ist die Nutzung eines neuen und verbesserten Faktors der Dezentralisierung, insbesondere der fiskalen Dezentralisierung. Dieser beachtet die reale Steuerautonomie, indem er nur Steuern berücksichtigt, über die die regionalen und lokalen Regierungen unabhängige legislative und administrative Gewalt besitzen.

Der Beitrag dieser Arbeit ist zweigeteilt. Einerseits erweitert sie die Literatur zu den empirischen Faktoren der ausländischen Direktinvestitionen, andererseits ergänzt sie die zahlreichen gut fundierten Anwendungen der Dezentralisierungstheorie. Zwei Hauptergebnisse verdeutlicht die Analyse im Kapitel 3. Erstens haben Grad und Stufe der Dezentralisierung in dem Gastland einen robusten negativen Effekt auf die Investitionsentscheidung. Im Einzelnen bescheinigt die Zahl der Regierungsebenen, das Messinstrument für die Bürokratie und administrative Struktur der Regierung, einen starken negativen Einfluss auf Fremddirektinvestitionen. Dieses Ergebnis kann mit der "Hold-up"-Problematik im Kontext von ausländischen Investitionen erklärt werden.

Die theoretische Literatur zur Thematik der Dezentralisierung und vorangegangene empirische Beweise belegen gemischte Ergebnisse über den Effekt der fiskalen Dezentralisierung. Dieses Kapitel findet jedoch einen bestehenden negativen Einfluss für den Grad der Steuerautonomie und Ausgabendezentralisierung, die als Messgrößen der fiskalen Dezentralisierung dienen. Das

Ergebnis kann mit Hilfe neuerer theoretischer Literatur zum Steuerwettbewerb erklärt werden. Darin wird die Ineffizienz als Ergebnis von Steuer- und Regulierungsüberlappungen zwischen den unterschiedlichen Regierungsebenen hervorgehoben.

Das zweite Ergebnis ist, dass die fiskale Dezentralisierung eine U-formige Auswirkung auf die ausländischen Investitionen haben kann. Das Minimum der Funktion liegt an einem verhältnismäßig hohen Grad der Steuerautonomie, der jedoch nur in vier der Länder in der Analyse vorhanden ist. Die Erklärung für die abnehmende Intensität der negativen Auswirkung von fiskaler Dezentralisierung, nachdem ein bestimmtes Niveau an Dezentralisierung erreicht ist, liegt im Prinzip der klaren Trennung der Gewalten zwischen föderalen, regionalen und lokalen Ebenen.

Nation Branding und ausländische Direktinvestitionen. Kapitel 4 ist durch Zusammenarbeit mit Prof. Dr. Kai A. Konrad entstanden. Während das vorangegangene Kapitel darlegte, dass ausländische Direktinvestitionen durch Dezentralisierung und andere ökonomische und geographische Faktoren gesteuert werden, geht Kapitel 4 der Frage nach, ob immaterielle ("intangible") Faktoren wie Länderstereotypen oder Verbrauchereinstellungen über die Produkte aus diesen Ländern ebenfalls eine Auswirkung auf die Investitionen haben. Diese Frage ist von Bedeutung für die Formulierung von politischen Regierungsstrategien. Schließlich wird die Wahrnehmung eines Landes zum großen Teil und somit auch sein Image in der Welt durch seine Regierungen und deren Handlungen bestimmt.

Die empirische Analyse im Kapitel 4 nutzt das empirische "Knowledge-Capital"-Modell, wie von Carr et al. (2001) entwickelt und von Davies (2008) erweitert wurde. Sie umfasst 30 Gastländer und 34 Investorenländer über einen Zeitraum von zwei Jahren 2005-2006. Diese Arbeit ist in vielerlei Hinsicht innovativ: Erstens untersucht sie eine Fragestellung, die nicht in der empirischen Literatur zu multinationalen Unternehmen bearbeitet wurde. Zweitens operationalisiert sie die "intangibles" eines Landes mit seinem Landesimage ("Nation Brand"). Drittens unternimmt diese Arbeit den Versuch Einsichten aus der Marketingtheorie mit der Empirie zu internationalem Handel zu verknüpfen.

Das Konzept zum Nation Brand(-ing) eines Landes steht im direkten Zusammenhang mit der Bedeutung und dem Verständnis zur spezifischen Originalität und somit auch zur Qualität des Landes sowohl für seine Industrie- wie auch Verbraucherprodukte. Die Marke des Herstellungslandes dient zugleich als Aushängeschild für dieses Land und die Qualität seiner Produkte und Arbeit und hat oft maßgeblichen Einfluss auf Entscheidungen für oder gegen den Konsum von Produkten aus diesem Land. Berücksichtigt man die Rolle, die das Herstellungsland (”country of origin”) und vor allem dessen Image bei der Entscheidungsfindung spielt, sollten die Vorteile und Vorzüge eines Herstellungslandes einen maßgeblichen Einfluss für multinationale Investoren haben, wenn es darum geht, ihren Produktionsstandort zu wählen. Es liegt daher nahe, sich für einen Produktionsstandort zu entscheiden, den der Verbraucher mit positiven Attributen bezüglich Herstellung und Qualität in Verbindung bringt. In gleichem Maße liefert das Image eines Landes Informationen zu dessen Qualitäten und Vorzüge für mögliche Investitionen.

Diese Einsichten führen zum folgenden Hauptergebnis der Analyse. Der Umfang von ausländischen Investitionen im Gastland steigt um 27 Prozent an, sobald sein Image bzw. seine ”intangibles” sich um einen Punkt verbessern. Des Weiteren berücksichtigt der Index die unterschiedliche Gewichtung bei der Erklärung der in das Land einfließenden Direktinvestitionen und ist nicht gesteuert durch fundamentalen oder ökonomischen Faktoren. Die herausragende Bedeutung und der beeindruckende positive Effekt des Nation Brand auf die Fremddirektinvestitionen kann als wichtige Motivation für Regierungen dienen, in eine Verbesserung ihres Landesimage zu investieren, um erfolgreich im Wettbewerb um ausländische Direktinvestitionen zu bestehen.

Bibliography

[1] Acemoglu, D. (2005). "Constitutions, Politics and Economics; A Review Essay on Persson and Tabellini's 'The Economic Effects of Constitutions'", Journal of Economic Literature, 43, 1025–1048.

[2] Aitken, N.D. (1973). "The Effect of the EEC and EFTA on European Trade: A Temporal Cross-Secion Analysis", American Economic Review, 63, 881-892.

[3] Alesina, A. and E. Spolaore (2003). *The Size of Nations*, The MIT Press.

[4] Alesina, A; E. Spolaore, and R. Wacziarg (2000). "Economic Integration and Political Disintegration", American Economic Review, 90, 1276-1296.

[5] Anderson, J.E. (1979). "A Theoretical Foundation for the Gravity Equation", American Economic Review, 69, 106-116.

[6] Anderson, J.E. and J.P. Neary (2003). "The Mercantilist Index of Trade Policy", International Economic Review, 44, 627-249.

[7] Anderson, J.E. and E. van Wincoop (2003). "Gravity with Gravitas: A Solution to the Border Puzzle", American Economic Review, 93, 170-192.

[8] Anderson, J.E. and E. van Wincoop (2004). "Trade costs", The Journal of Economic Literature, XLII, 691-751.

[9] Anholt, S. (2005). Anholt-GMI Nation Brands Index 2005q1, earthspeak.com.

[10] Arzaghi, M. and J.V. Henderson (2005). "Why Countries Are Fiscally Decentralizing," Journal of Public Economics, 89, 1157-1189.

[11] Baier, S.L. and J.H. Bergstrand (2007). "Do Free Trade Agreements Actually Increase Members' International Trade?", Journal of International Economics, 71, 72-95.

[12] Baier, S.L. and J.H. Bergstrand (2009). "Bonus Vetus OLS: A Simple Method for Approximating International Trade-Cost Effects Using the Gravity Equation," Journal of International Economics, 77, 77-85.

[13] Bardhan, P. (2002). "Decentralization of Governance and Development," Journal of Economic Perspectives, 16(4), 185-205.

[14] Benassy-Quere, A.; L. Fontagne and A. Lahreche-Revil (2005). "How Does FDI React to Corporate Taxation?", International Tax and Public Finance, 12, 583-603.

[15] Bergstrand, J.H. (1985). "The Gravity Equation in International Trade: Some Microeconomic Foundations and Empirical Evidence", Review of Economics and Statistics, 67, 474-481.

[16] Bergstrand, J.H. (1989). "The Generalized Gravity Equation Monopolistic Competition, and the Factor-Proportions Theory in International Trade", Review of Economics and Statistics, 71, 143-153.

[17] Berkowitz, D. and W. Li (2000). "Tax Rights in Transition Economies: A Tragedy of the Commons?," Journal of Public Economics, 76, 369-397.

[18] Bilkey, W.J. and E. Nes (1982). "Country-of-Origin Effects on Product Evaluations", Journal of International Business Studies, 13 (1), 89-99.

[19] Blonigen, B.A. (2005). "A Review of the Empirical Literature on FDI Determinants", Atlantic Economic Journal, 33, 383-403.

[20] Blonigen, B.A and R.B. Davies (2004). "The Effects of Bilateral Tax Treaties on U.S. FDI Activity", International Tax and Public Finance, 11 (5), 601-622.

[21] Blonigen, B.A., R.B. Davies, and K. Head (2003). "Estimating the Knowledge-Capital Model of the Multinational Enterprise: Comment", American Economic Review, 93 (3), 980-994.

[22] Blonigen, B.A.; R.B. Davies, G.R. Waddell, and H.T. Naughton (2007). "FDI in Space: Spatial Autoregressive Relationships in Foreign Direct Investment", European Economic Review, 51, 1303-1325.

[23] Boadway, R.; S. Roberts and A. Shah (1994). "The Reform of Fiscal Systems in Developing and Emerging Market Economies", World Bank Policy Research Working Paper 1259.

[24] Braconier, H.; P.-J. Norbäck and D. Urban (2005). "Reconciling the Evidence on the Knowledge-Capital Model", Review of International Economics, 13, 770-786.

[25] Brainard, S.L. (1997). "An empirical assessment of the proximity concentration tradeoff between multinational sales and trade," American Economic Review, 87(4), 520-544.

[26] Brandeis, L. (1932). *Dissent on New State Ice Co. v. Liebman*, 285 U.S. 262.

[27] Brennan, G. and J.M. Buchanan (1980). *The Power to Tax: Analytical Foundations of a Fiscal Constitution*, Cambridge University Press, Cambridge.

[28] Carr, D.L.; J.R. Markusen and K.E. Maskus (2001). "Estimating the Knowledge-Capital Model of the Multinational Enterprise", American Economic Review, 91 (3), 693-708.

[29] Carr, D.L.; J.R. Markusen and K.E. Maskus (2003). "Estimating the Knowledge-Capital Model of the Multinational Enterprise: Reply", American Economic Review, 93 (3), 995-1001.

[30] Chen, N. (2004). "Intra-National versus International Trade in the European Union: Why Do National Borders Matter?", Journal of International Economics, 63, 93-118.

[31] Daude, C. and E. Stein (2007). "The Quality of Institutions and Foreign Direct Investment", Economics and Politics, 19 (3), 317-344.

[32] Davies, R.B. (2008). "Hunting High and Low for Vertical FDI", Review of International Economics, 16 (2), 250-267.

[33] Deardorff, A.V. (1998). "Determinants of Bilateral Trade: Does Gravity Work in a Neoclassical World?" in *The Regionalization of the World Economy*, ed. J.A. Frankel, Chicago: University of Chicago Press.

[34] Deardorff, A.V. and R.M. Stern (1998). *Measurement of Nontariff Barriers*, Ann Arbor: University of Michigan Press.

[35] Devereux, M.P.; R. Griffith and A. Klemm (2002). "Corporate income tax reforms and international tax competition", Economic Policy, 35, 451-495.

[36] Disdier, A.-C. and K. Head (2008). "The Puzzling Persistence of the Distance Effect on Bilateral Trade", Review of Economics and Statistics, 90, 37-48.

[37] Djankov, S.; R. La Porta, F. López-de-Silanes and A. Shleifer (2002). "The Regulation of Entry", Quarterly Journal of Economics, 117 (1), 1-37.

[38] Donahue, J.D. (1997). "Tiebout? Or Not Tiebout? The Market Metaphor and America's Devolution Debate", Journal of Economic Perspectives, 11, 73-81.

[39] Egger, P. and M. Pfaffermayr (2004). "The Impact of Bilateral Investment Treaties on Foreign Direct Investment", Journal of Comparative Economics, 32, 788-804.

[40] Eichengreen, B. and D.A. Irwin (1998). "The Role of History in Bilateral Trade Flows," NBER Chapters, in *The Regionalization of the World Economy*, 33-62, National Bureau of Economic Research, Inc.

[41] Ekholm, K.; R. Forslid and J.R. Markusen (2007). "Export-Platform Foreign Direct Investment," Journal of the European Economic Association, 5, 776-795.

[42] Enikolopov, R. and E. Zhuravskaya (2007). "Decentralization and Political Institutions", Journal of Public Economics, 91, 2261-2290.

[43] Evans, C.L. (2003). "The Economic Significance of National Border Effects", American Economic Review, 93 (4), 1291-1312.

[44] Evenett, S. and W. Keller (2002). "On Theories Explaining the Success of the Gravity Equation", Journal of Political Economy, 110, 281-316.

[45] Fan, Y. (2006). "Branding the Nation: What Is Being Branded?", Journal of Vacation Marketing, 12 (1), 5-14.

[46] Feenstra, R.C. (2002). "Border Effects and the Gravity Equation: Consistent Methods for Estimation", Scottish Journal of Political Economy, 49, 491-506.

[47] Feenstra, R.C.; J.A. Markusen and A.K. Rose (2001). "Using the Gravity Equation to Differentiate among Alternative Theories of Trade", Canadian Journal of Economics, 34, 430-447.

[48] Feinberg, S.E. and M.P. Keene (2001). "U.S.-Canada Trade Liberalization and MNC Production Location", Review of Economics and Statistics, 83, 118-132.

[49] Fisman, R. and R. Gatti (2002). "Decentralization and Corruption: Evidence Across Countries", Journal of Public Economics, 83(3), 325-345.

[50] Frankel, J.A; E. Stein and S.J. Wei (1997). *Regional Trading Blocs in the World Economic System*, Washington, DC: Institute for International Economics.

[51] Gao, T. (2003). "Ethnic Chinese Networks and International Investment: Evidence from Inward FDI in China", Journal of Asian Economics, 14 (4), 611-629.

[52] Graham, E.M. and P.R. Krugman (1989). *Foreign Direct Investment in the United States*, Institute for International Economics, Washington, DC.

[53] Harrigan, J. (1993). "Scale Economics and the Volume of Trade", Review of Economics and Statistics, 76, 321-328.

[54] Haveman, J and D. Hummels (2004). "Alternative Hypotheses and the Volume of Trade: The Gravity Equation and the Extent of Specialization", Canadian Journal of Economics, 37, 199-218.

[55] Hayek, F. (1945). "The Use of Knowledge in Society", Americal Economic Review, 35, 519-530

[56] Head, K. and T. Mayer (2002). "Illusory Border Effects: Distance Mismeasurement Inflates Estimates of Home Bias in Trade", CEPII Working Paper 2002-01.

[57] Helliwell, J.F. (1996). "Do National Borders Matter for Quebec's Trade", Canadian Journal of Economics, 29, 507-522.

[58] Helliwell, J.F. (1997). "National Borders, Trade and Migration", Pacific Economic Review, 3, 165-185.

[59] Helliwell, J.F. and G. Verdier (2001). "Measuring Internal Trade Distances: A New Method Applied to Estimate Provincial Border Effects in Canada", Canadian Journal of Economics. 34, 1024-1041.

[60] Helpman, E. (1984). "A Simple Theory of International Trade with Multinational Corporations", Journal of Political Economy, 92 (3), 451-471.

[61] Helpman, E. and P. Krugman (1985), *Market Structure and Foreign Trade*, Cambridge, MA: MIT Press.

[62] Helpman, A.; M. Melitz and Y. Rubinstein (2008). "Estimating Trade Flows: Trading Partners and Trading Volumes", Quarterly Journal of Economics, 123, 441-487.

[63] Helpman, A.; M.J. Melitz and S.R.Yeaple (2004). "Export Versus FDI with Heterogenous Firms", American Economic Review, 94, 300-316.

[64] Hong, S.-T. and R.S. Wyer, Jr. (1989). "Effects of Country-of-Origin and Product-Attribute Information on Product Evaluation: An Information Processing Perspective", Journal of Consumer Research, 16 (2), 175-187.

[65] Horstmann, I.J. and J.R. Markusen (1987). "Strategic Investments and the Development of Multinationals", International Economic Review, 28, 109-121.

[66] Horstmann, I.J. and J.R. Markusen (1992). "Endogenous Market Structures in International Trade (nature facit saltum)", Journal of International Economics, 32, 109-129.

[67] Hummels, D. (1999). "Have International Transportation Costs Declined?", mimeo.

[68] Hummels, D. (2001). "Toward a Geography of Trade Costs", mimeo.

[69] Inman, R.P. and D.L. Rubinfeld (1997). "Rethinking Federalism", Journal of Economic Perspectives, 11, 43-64.

[70] Jamarchik, S. and S. Ghosh (2005). "A Sensitivity Analysis of the Gravity Model", The International Trade Journal, 19, 83-126.

[71] Johansson, J.K.; S.P. Douglas and I. Nonaka (1985). "Assessing the Impact of Country of Origin on Product Evaluations: A New Methodological Perspective", Journal of Marketing Research, 22 (4), 388-396.

[72] Kalamova, M.M. (2008). "Decentralization and Foreign Direct Investment: Evidence from the OECD Countries", mimeo.

[73] Kaufmann, D.; A. Kraay and M. Mastruzzi (2008). "Governance Matters VII: Aggregate and Individual Governance Indicators for 1996 - 2007", Policy Research Working Paper Series 4654, World Bank.

[74] Keen, M. (1998). "Vertical Tax Externalities in the Theory of Fiscal Federalism", International Monetary Fund Stuff Papers, 45.

[75] Keen, M. and C. Kotsogiannis (2002). "Does Federalism Lead to Excessively High Taxes?", American Economic Review, 92, 363-370.

[76] Kessing, S.G.; K.A. Konrad, and C. Kotsogiannis (2006). "Federal Tax Autonomy and the Limits of Cooperation", Journal of Urban Economics, 59, 317-329.

[77] Kessing, S.G.; K.A. Konrad, and C. Kotsogiannis (2007). "Foreign Direct Investment and the Dark Side of Decentralization", Economic Policy, 22 (49), 6-70.

[78] Kessing, S.G.; K.A. Konrad, and C. Kotsogiannis (2009). "Fedrealism, weak institutions and the competition for foreign direct investment," International Tax and Public Finance, 16, 105-123.

[79] Klein, J.G. (2002). "Us versus Them, or Us versus Everyone? Delineating Consumer Aversion to Foreign Goods", Journal of International Business Studies, 33 (2), 345-363.

[80] Li, W.-K. and R.S. Wyer, Jr. (1994). "The Role of Country of Origin in Product Evaluations: Informational and Standard-of-Comparison Effects", Journal of Consumer Psychology, 3 (2), 187-212.

[81] Maheswaran, D. (1994). "Country of Origin as a Stereotype: Effects of Consumer Expertise and Attribute Strength on Product Evaluations", Journal of Consumer Research, 21 (2), 354-365.

[82] Markusen, J.R. (1984). "Multinationals, Multi-Plant Economies, and the Gains from Trade", Journal of International Economics, 16 (3-4), 205-226.

[83] Markusen, J.R. (2002). *Multinational Firms and the Theory of International Trade*, Cambridge, MA: MIT Press.

[84] Markusen, J.R. and K.E. Maskus (2002). "Discriminating Among Alternative Theories of the Multinational Enterprise", Review of International Economics, 10 (4), 694-707.

[85] Markusen, J.R. and A. Venables (1998). "Trade Policy with Increasing Returns and Imperfect Competition: Contradictory Results from Competing Assumptions", Journal of International Economics, 24, 299-316.

[86] Markusen, J.R. and A. Venables (2000). "The Theory of Endowment, Intra-Industry and Multinational Trade", Journal of International Economics, 52, 209-235.

[87] Mauro, P. (1995). "Corruption and Growth", Quarterly Journal of Economics, 110 (3), 681-712.

[88] McCallum, J. (1995). "National Borders Matter: Canada-U.S. Regional Trade Patterns", American Economic Review, 85, 615-623.

[89] McDonald, J.F. and R.A. Moffitt (1980). "The uses of tobit analysis", Review of Economics and Statistics, 62 (2), 318– 321.

[90] Melitz, M.J. (2003). "The Impact of Trade on Intra-Industry Reallocations and Aggregate Industry Productivity", Econometrica, 71, 1695-1725.

[91] Messerlin, P. (2001). *Measuring the Cost of Protection in Europe*, Washington, DC: Institute for International Economics.

[92] Musgrave, R.M. (1959). *The Theory of Public Finance*, NY: McGraw-Hill.

[93] Nitsch, V. (2000). "National Borders and International Trade: Evidence from the European Union", Canadian Journal of Economics, 33(4), 1091-1105.

[94] Oates, W.E. (1972). "Fiscal Federalism", Harcourt-Brace, New York.

[95] Oates, W.E. (1999). "An Essay on Fiscal Federalism", Journal of Economic Literature, 1120-1149.

[96] OECD (1999). "Taxing Powers of State and Local Government", OECD Tax Policy Studies No.1, Paris.

[97] Panizza, U. (1999). "On the Determinants of Fiscal Centralization: Theory and Evidence", Journal of Public Economics, 74(1), 97-139.

[98] Peterson, R.A. and A.J.P. Jolibert (1995). "A Meta-Analysis of Country-of-Origin Effects", Journal of International Business Studies, 26 (4), 883-900.

[99] Prud'homme, R. (1995). "On the Dangers of Decentralization", World Bank Research Observer, 10, 201-220.

[100] Qian, Y. and G. Roland (1998). "Federalism and the Soft Budget Constraint", Americal Economic Review, 88, 1143-1162.

[101] Qian, Y. and B.R. Weingast (1997). "Federalism as a Commitment to Preserving Market Incentives", Journal of Economic Perspectives, 11, 83-92.

[102] Riker, W. (1964). *Federalism: Origins, Operation, Significance*, Boston, MA: Little, Brown and Co.

[103] Rose, A.K. (2004). "Do We Really Know that the WTO Increases Trade?", American Economic Review, 94 (1), 98-114.

[104] Rousseau, J.J. (1976). *The Social Contract in Political Writings*, translated and edited by Frederick Watkins, Madison, University of Washington Press, 1986.

[105] Samiee, S. (1994). "Customer Evaluation of Products in a Global Market", Journal of International Business Studies, 25 (3), 579-604.

[106] Samiee, S.; T.A. Shimp and S. Sharma (2005). "Brand Origin Recognition Accuracy: Its Antecedents and Consumers' Cognitive Limitations", Journal of International Business Studies, 36 (4), 379-397.

[107] Seabright, P. (1995). "Accountability and Decentralization in Government: An Incomplete Contracts Model", European Economic Review, 40, 61-89.

[108] Shah, A. (2008). "Macro Federalism and Local Finance", Public Setor Governance and Accountability Series, World Bank.

[109] Shleifer, A. and R. Vishny (1993). "Corruption", Quarterly Journal of Economics, 108(3), 599-617.

[110] Stegarescu, D. (2005). "Public Sector Decentralisation: Measurement Concepts and Recent International Trends", Fiscal Studies 26(3), 301-333.

[111] Stegarescu, D. (2006). *Decentralised Government in an Integrating World: Quantitative Studies for OECD Countries*, ZEW Economic Studies, Physica-Verlag.

[112] Stein, E. and C. Daude (2007). "Longitude Matters: Time Zones and the Location of Foreign Direct Investment", Journal of International Economics, 71 (1), 96-112.

[113] Subramanian, A. and S.-J. Wei (2007). "The WTO Promotes Trade, Strongly but Unevenly", Journal of International Economics, 72, 151-175.

[114] Tanzi, V. (1995). "Fiscal Federalism and Decentralization: A Review of Some Efficiency and Macroeconomic Aspects," Paper presented at Annual World Bank Conference on Development Economics, 295-316.

[115] Tanzi, V. (2000). "On Fiscal Federalism: Issues to Worry About", paper presented at an IMF conference, November, Washington D.C.

[116] Tiebout, C. (1956). "A Pure Theory of Local Expenditures", Journal of Political Economy, 64, 416-424.

[117] Tinbergen, J. (1962). *Shaping the World Economy*, New York: The Twentieth Century Fund.

[118] Treisman, D. (2002). "Decentralization and the Quality of Government", mimeo, University of California, Los Angeles.

[119] Treisman, D. (2007). "The Architecture of Government", Cambridge University Press.

[120] Tse, D.K. and W. Lee (1993). "Removing Negative Country Images: Effects of Decomposition, Branding, and Product Experience", Journal of International Marketing, 1 (4), 25-48.

[121] Verlegh, P.W.J. and J.-B.E.M Steenkamp (1999). "A Review and Meta-Analysis of Country-of-Origin Research", Journal of Economic Psychology, 20 (5), 521-546.

[122] Wei, S.-J. (1996). "Intra-National versus International Trade: How Stubborn Are Nations in Global Integration?", National Bureau of Economic Research Working Paper 5939.

[123] Wei, S.-J. (2000). "How Taxing Is Corruption on International Investors?", Review of Economics and Statistics, 82 (1), 1-11.

[124] Weingast, B.R. (1995). "The Economic Role of Political Institutions: Market-Preserving Federalism and Economic Development", Journal of Law, Economics and Organization, 11, 1-31.

[125] Wilson, J. D. (1986). A theory of interregional tax competition, Journal of Urban Economics 19, 296-315.

[126] Wilson, J. D. (1999). Theories of tax competition. National Tax Journal 52, 269-304.

[127] Wolf, H.C. (2000). "Intranational Home Bias in Trade", Review of Economics and Statistics, 82, 555-563.

[128] World Bank (2000). "Entering the 21st Century", World Development Report 1999/2000, New York: Oxford University Press.

[129] Wooldridge, J. (2002). "Econometric Analysis of Cross Section and Panel Data", MIT Press.

[130] Wrede, M. (1997). "Tax Competition and Federalism: The Underprovision of Local Public Goods", FinanzArchiv, 54, 494-515.

[131] Wrede, M. (2000). "Shared Tax Sources and Public Expenditures", International Tax and Public Finance, 7, 163-175.

[132] WTO (2006). "World Trade 2005, Prospects for 2006", Press/437, 2006 Press Releases.

[133] Yeaple, S.R. (2003). "The Role of Skill Endowments in the Structure of U.S. Outward Foreign Direct Investment", Review of Economics and Statistics, 85, 726-734.

[134] Zodrow, G. R. and P. Mieszkowski (1986). "Pigou, Tiebout, property taxation, and the underprovision of local public goods", Journal of Urban Economics, 19, 356-370.

FINANZWISSENSCHAFTLICHE SCHRIFTEN

Band 1 Werner Steden: Finanzpolitik und Einkommensverteilung. Ein Wachstums- und Konjunkturmodell der Bundesrepublik Deutschland. 1979.

Band 2 Rainer Hagemann: Kommunale Finanzplanung im föderativen Staat. 1976.

Band 3 Klaus Scherer: Maßstäbe zur Beurteilung von konjunkturellen Wirkungen des öffentlichen Haushalts. 1977.

Band 4 Brita Steinbach: „Formula Flexibility" - Kritische Analyse und Vergleich mit diskretionärer Konjunkturpolitik. 1977.

Band 5 Hans-Georg Petersen: Personelle Einkommensbesteuerung und Inflation. Eine theoretisch-empirische Analyse der Lohn- und veranlagten Einkommensteuer in der Bundesrepublik Deutschland. 1977.

Band 6 Friedemann Tetsch: Raumwirkungen des Finanzsystems der Bundesrepublik Deutschland. Eine Untersuchung der Auswirkungen der Finanzreform von 1969 auf die Einnahmenposition der untergeordneten Gebietskörperschaften und ihrer regionalpolitischen Zieladäquanz. 1978.

Band 7 Wilhelm Pfähler: Normative Theorie der fiskalischen Besteuerung. Ein methodologischer und theoretischer Beitrag zur Integration der normativen Besteuerungstheorie in der Wohlfahrtstheorie. 1978.

Band 8 Wolfgang Wiegard: Optimale Schattenpreise und Produktionsprogramme für öffentliche Unternehmen. Second-Best Modelle im finanzwirtschaftlichen Staatsbereich. 1978.

Band 9 Hans P. Fischer: Die Finanzierung des Umweltschutzes im Rahmen einer rationalen Umweltpolitik. 1978.

Band 10 Rainer Paulenz: Der Einsatz finanzpolitischer Instrumente in der Forschungs- und Entwicklungspolitik. 1978.

Band 11 Hans-Joachim Hauser: Verteilungswirkungen der Staatsverschuldung. Eine kreislauftheoretische Inzidenzbetrachtung. 1979.

Band 12 Gunnar Schwarting: Kommunale Investitionen. Theoretische und empirische Untersuchungen der Bestimmungsgründe kommunaler Investitionstätigkeit in Nordrhein-Westfalen 1965-1972. 1979.

Band 13 Hans-Joachim Conrad: Stadt-Umland-Wanderung und Finanzwirtschaft der Kernstädte. Amerikanische Erfahrungen, grundsätzliche Zusammenhänge und eine Fallstudie für das Ballungsgebiet Frankfurt am Main. 1980.

Band 14 Cay Folkers: Vermögensverteilung und staatliche Aktivität. Zur Theorie distributiver Prozesse im Interventionsstaat. 1981.

Band 15 Helmut Fischer: US-amerikanische Exportförderung durch die DISC-Gesetzgebung. 1981.

Band 16 Günter Ott: Einkommensumverteilungen in der gesetzlichen Krankenversicherung. Eine quantitative Analyse. 1981.

Band 17 Johann Hermann von Oehsen: Optimale Besteuerung. *(Optimal Taxation)*. 1982.

Band 18 Richard Kössler: Sozialversicherungsprinzip und Staatszuschüsse in der gesetzlichen Rentenversicherung. 1982.

Band 19 Hinrich Steffen: Zum Handlungs- und Entscheidungsspielraum der kommunalen Investitionspolitik in der Bundesrepublik Deutschland. 1983.

Band 20 Manfred Scheuer: Wirkungen einer Auslandsverschuldung des Staates bei flexiblen Wechselkursen. 1983.

Band 21 Christian Schiller: Staatsausgaben und crowding-out-Effekte. Zur Effizienz einer Finanzpolitik keynesianischer Provenienz. 1983.

Band 22 Hannelore Weck: Schattenwirtschaft: Eine Möglichkeit zur Einschränkung der öffentlichen Verwaltung? Eine ökonomische Analyse. 1983.

Band 23 Wolfgang Schmitt: Steuern als Mittel der Einkommenspolitik. Eine Ergänzung der Stabilitätspolitik? 1984.

Band 24 Wolfgang Laux: Erhöhung staatswirtschaftlicher Effizienz durch budgetäre Selbstbeschränkung? Zur Idee einer verfassungsmäßig verankerten Ausgabengrenze. 1984.

Band 25 Brita Steinbach-van der Veen: Steuerinzidenz. Methodologische Grundlagen und empirisch-statistische Probleme von Länderstudien. 1985.

Band 26 Albert Peters: Ökonomische Kriterien für eine Aufgabenverteilung in der Marktwirtschaft. Eine deskriptive und normative Betrachtung für den Allokationsbereich. 1985.

Band 27 Achim Zeidler: Möglichkeiten zur Fortsetzung der Gemeindefinanzreform. Eine theoretische und empirische Analyse. 1985.

Band 28 Peter Bartsch: Zur Theorie der längerfristigen Wirkungen ‚expansiver' Fiskalpolitik. Eine dynamische Analyse unter besonderer Berücksichtigung der staatlichen Budgetbeschränkung und ausgewählter Möglichkeiten der öffentlichen Defizitfinanzierung. 1986.

Band 29 Konrad Beiwinkel: Wehrgerechtigkeit als finanzpolitisches Verteilungsproblem. Möglichkeiten einer Kompensation von Wehrungerechtigkeit durch monetäre Transfers. 1986.

Band 30 Wolfgang Kitterer: Effizienz- und Verteilungswirkungen des Steuersystems. 1986.

Band 31 Heinz Dieter Hessler: Theorie und Politik der Personalsteuern. Eine Kritik ihrer Einkommens- und Vermögensbegriffe mit Blick auf die Leistungsfähigkeitstheorie. 1994.

Band 32 Wolfgang Scherf: Die beschäftigungspolitische und fiskalische Problematik der Arbeitgeberbeiträge zur Rentenversicherung. Eine Auseinandersetzung mit der Kritik an der lohnbezogenen Beitragsbemessung. 1987.

Band 33 Andreas Mästle: Die Steuerunion. Probleme der Harmonisierung spezifischer Gütersteuern. 1987.

Band 34 Günter Ott: Internationale Verteilungswirkungen im Finanzausgleich der Europäischen Gemeinschaften. 1987.

Band 35 Heinz Haller: Zur Frage der zweckmäßigen Gestalt gemeindlicher Steuern. Ein Diskussionsbeitrag zur Gemeindesteuerreform. 1987.

Band 36 Thomas Kuhn: Schlüsselzuweisungen und fiskalische Ungleichheit. Eine theoretische Analyse der Verteilung von Schlüsselzuweisungen an Kommunen. 1988.

Band 37 Walter Hahn: Steuerpolitische Willensbildungsprozesse in der Europäischen Gemeinschaft. Das Beispiel der Umsatzssteuer-Harmonisierung. 1988.

Band 38 Ulrike Hardt: Kommunale Finanzkraft. Die Problematik einer objektiven Bestimmung kommunaler Einnahmemöglichkeiten in der gemeindlichen Haushaltsplanung und im kommunalen Finanzausgleich. 1988.

Band 39 Jochen Michaelis: Optimale Finanzpolitik im Modell überlappender Generationen. 1989.

Band 40 Bernd Raffelhüschen: Anreizwirkungen der sozialen Alterssicherung. Eine dynamische Simulationsanalyse. 1989.

Band 41 Berend Diekmann: Die Anleihe- und Darlehenstransaktionen der Europäischen Gemeinschaften. 1990.

Band 42 Helmut Kaiser: Konsumnachfrage, Arbeitsangebot und optimale Haushaltsbesteuerung. Theoretische Ergebnisse und mikroökonometrische Simulation für die Bundesrepublik Deutschland. 1990.

Band 43 Rüdiger von Kleist: Das Gramm-Rudman-Hollings-Gesetz. Ein gescheiterter Versuch der Haushaltskonsolidierung. 1991.

Band 44 Rolf Hagedorn: Steuerhinterziehung und Finanzpolitik. Ein theoretischer Beitrag unter besonderer Berücksichtigung der Hinterziehung von Zinserträgen. 1991.

Band 45 Cornelia S. Behrens: Intertemporale Verteilungswirkungen in der gesetzlichen Krankenversicherung der Bundesrepublik Deutschland. 1991.

Band 46 Peter Saile: Ein ökonomischer Ansatz der Theorie der intermediären Finanzgewalten – Die Kirchen als Parafisci. 1992.

Band 47 Peter Gottfried: Die verdeckten Effizienzwirkungen der Umsatzsteuer. Eine empirische allgemeine Gleichgewichtsanalyse. 1992.

Band 48 Andreas Burger: Umweltorientierte Beschäftigungsprogramme. Eine Effizienzanalyse am Beispiel des „Sondervermögens Arbeit und Umwelt". 1992.

Band 49 Jeanette Malchow: Die Zuordnung verteilungspolitischer Kompetenzen in der Europäischen Gemeinschaft. Eine Untersuchung aufgrund einer Fortentwicklung der ökonomischen Theorie des Föderalismus. 1992.

Band 50 Barbara Seidel: Die Einbindung der Bundesrepublik Deutschland in die Europäischen Gemeinschaften als Problem des Finanzausgleichs. 1992.

Band 51 Ralph Wiechers: Markt und Macht im Rundfunk. Zur Stellung der öffentlich-rechtlichen Rundfunkanstalten im dualen Rundfunksystem der Bundesrepublik Deutschland. 1992.

Band 52 Klaus Eckhardt: Probleme einer Umweltpolitik mit Abgaben. 1993.

Band 53 Oliver Schwarzkopf: Die Problematik unterschiedlicher Körperschaftsteuersysteme innerhalb der EG. 1993.

Band 54 Thorsten Giersch: Bergson-Wohlfahrtsfunktion und normative Ökonomie. 1993.

Band 55 Li-Fang Chou: Selbstbeteiligung bei Arzneimitteln aus ordnungspolitischer Sicht. Das Beispiel der Bundesrepublik Deutschland. 1993.

Band 56 Harald Schlee: Einkommensteuerliche Behandlung von Transferzahlungen. Zur Neuordnung der Familienbesteuerung sowie der Besteuerung von Versicherungsleistungen und Sozialtransfers. 1994.

Band 57 Alexander Spermann: Kommunales Krisenmanagement. Reaktionen baden-württembergischer Stadtkreise auf steigende Sozialhilfekosten und Einnahmenausfälle (1980- 92). 1993.

Band 58 Otto Roloff / Sibylle Brander / Ingo Barens / Claudia Wesselbaum: Direktinvestitionen und internationale Steuerkonkurrenz. 1994.

Band 59 Claudia Wesselbaum-Neugebauer: Internationale Steuerbelastungsvergleiche. 1994.

Band 60 Stephanie Miera: Kommunales Finanzsystem und Bevölkerungsentwicklung. Eine Analyse des kommunalen Finanzsystems vor dem Hintergrund der sich abzeichnenden Bevölkerungsentwicklung am Beispiel Niedersachsens unter besonderer Berücksichtigung des Landkreises Wolfenbüttel und seiner Gemeinden. 1994.

Band 61 Wolfgang Scherf: Die Bedeutung des kaldorianischen Verteilungsmechanismus für die gesamtwirtschaftlichen Wirkungen der staatlichen Neuverschuldung. 1994.

Band 62 Rainer Volk: Vergleich der Vergünstigungseffekte der verschiedenen investitionsfördernden Maßnahmen. 1994.

Band 63 Hans-Georg Napp: Kommunale Finanzautonomie und ihre Bedeutung für eine effiziente lokale Finanzwirtschaft. 1994. 2., unveränderte Auflage 1994.

Band 64 Bernd Rahmann / Uwe Steinborn / Günter Vornholz: Empirische Analyse der Autonomie lokaler Finanzwirtschaften in der Europäischen Gemeinschaft. 1994.

Band 65 Carsten Kühl: Strategien zur Finanzierung der Altlastensanierung. 1994.

Band 66 Stephan Boll: Intergenerationale Umverteilungswirkungen der Fiskalpolitik in der Bundesrepublik Deutschland. Ein Ansatz mit Hilfe des Generational Accounting. 1994.

Band 67 Karl Justus Bernhard Neumärker: Finanzverfassung und Staatsgewalt in der Demokratie. Ein Beitrag zur konstitutionellen Finanztheorie. 1995.

Band 68 Christian Haslbeck: Zentrale versus dezentrale Internalisierung externer Effekte bei unvollständiger Information. 1995.

Band 69 Regina Müller: Horizontale oder vertikale Transfers zur Durchsetzung eines horizontalen Finanzausgleichs. 1995.

Band 70 Christian Hockenjos: Öffentliche Sportförderung in der Bundesrepublik Deutschland. Darstellung und finanztheoretische Analyse. 1995.

Band 71 Manfred Rosenstock: Die Kontrolle und Harmonisierung nationaler Beihilfen durch die Kommission der Europäischen Gemeinschaften. 1995.

Band 72 Christian Rüsch: Wohnungsbau- und Wohneigentumspolitik im Rahmen der Einkommensteuer. Eine Analyse unter steuersystematischen, verteilungspolitischen und fiskalischen Aspekten. 1996.

Band 73 Stephan Winters: Die kollektive Vorsorge für den Pflegefall im Alter. Eine Untersuchung am Beispiel der gesetzlichen Pflegeversicherung in den Niederlanden. 1996.

Band 74 Knut Blind: Allokationsineffizienzen auf Sicherheitsmärkten: Ursachen und Lösungsmöglichkeiten. Fallstudie: Informationssicherheit in Kommunikationssystemen. 1996.

Band 75 Barbara Petrick-Rump: Ökonomische Wirkungen von Steueramnestien. Untersuchung konkreter Erfahrungen ausgewählter Länder mit dem Einsatz von Steueramnestien anhand eines effizienten Steueramnestieprogramms. 1996.

Band 76 Georg Hirte: Effizienzwirkungen von Finanzausgleichsregelungen. Eine Empirische Allgemeine Gleichgewichtsanalyse für die Bundesrepublik Deutschland. 1996.

Band 77 Ulrike Kirchhoff: Die rheinland-pfälzischen Gemeinden im System des Finanzausgleichs. 1996.

Band 78 Kerstin Keil: Der soziale Mietwohnungsbau: Mängel und Alternativen. 1996.

Band 79 Bernhard Manzke: Kinderlastenausgleich versus verstärkte Einwanderung. Alternative Ansätze zur langfristigen Sicherung der Gesetzlichen Rentenversicherung. 1997.

Band 80 Hariolf M. Wenzler: Institutionenökonomik und öffentliche Finanzkontrolle. Eine Analyse am Beispiel der Europäischen Union. 1997.

Band 81 Joachim Nagel: Supply-Side Policy in den USA. Eine theoretische und empirische Analyse der angebotsorientierten Wirtschaftspolitik Reagans unter besonderer Berücksichtigung steuerlicher Aspekte. 1997.

Band 82 Heinz Lampert: Krise und Reform des Sozialstaates. 1997.

Band 83 Monika Hanswillemenke / Bernd Rahmann: Zwischen Reformen und Verantwortung für Vollbeschäftigung. Die Finanz- und Haushaltspolitik der sozial-liberalen Koalition von 1969 bis 1982. 1997.

Band 84 Berthold Fürst: Die Maastrichter Budgetkriterien im Konflikt mit der Verschuldungsautonomie der deutschen Gebietskörperschaften. 1997.

Band 85 Burkhard Pahnke: Einkommensorientierte Förderung des sozialen Mietwohnungsbaues. Bestandsaufnahme und Kritik. 1998.

Band 86 Judith Safford: Staatsverschuldung im Vereinigten Königreich. Die öffentliche Verschuldung unter der Konservativen Regierung von 1979-1994. Ursachen und Auswirkungen. 1998.

Band 87 Ralf Oberheide: Die Bekämpfung der Steuerumgehung. 1998.

Band 88 Achim Truger: Die neue Finanzwissenschaft zwischen Realitätsferne und Irrelevanz der Annahmen. Eine methodologische Analyse potentieller Verteidigungsstrategien der neuen Finanzwissenschaft gegen den Vorwurf der Realitätsferne ihres entscheidungstheoretischen Fundamentes. 1998.

Band 89 Karin Bickel: Familienbezogene Elemente im System der gesetzlichen Rentenversicherung. Unter besonderer Berücksichtigung von Ein-Eltern-Familien. 1999.

Band 90 Wolfgang Scherf: Schlüsselzuweisungen und Kreisumlage. Die Problematik der Finanzierung der Landkreise am Beispiel des kommunalen Finanzausgleichs von Rheinland-Pfalz. 1998.

Band 91 Sandra Ehmann: Familienpolitik in Frankreich und Deutschland – ein Vergleich. 1999.

Band 92 Hendrik Suermann: Einkommensteuerliche Behandlung von Währungsgewinnen und -verlusten. Eine finanzwissenschaftliche Analyse des Steuerrechts in den USA und in Deutschland. 1999.

Band 93 Rolf Bösinger: Die Neuordnung des bundesstaatlichen Finanzausgleichs 1995. Eine theoretische und empirische Analyse unter Berücksichtigung von allokationstheoretischen und polit-ökonomischen Gesichtspunkten. 1999.

Band 94 Ulrich Ermschel: Finanzwirtschaftliche Konsequenzen beim Übergang auf das Ursprungslandprinzip im Europäischen Binnenmarkt. Eine Untersuchung am Beispiel des unvollkommenen oligopolistischen Neufahrzeugmarktes. 1999.

Band 95 Ute Hansen: Überwälzte Leistungen der Administration. Eine empirische und theoretische Analyse. 2000.

Band 96 Hans-Werner Seiler: Zur Durchsetzung der Einmalbesteuerung deutscher Körperschaftsgewinne. Strategien zur Vermeidung der im deutschen Körperschaftsteuersystem angelegten Benachteiligung ausländischer Anteilseigner. Eine finanzwissenschaftliche Analyse. 2000.

Band 97 Steffen Meyer: Zwischenstaatliche Finanzzuweisungen im zusammenwachsenden Europa. Zur Gestaltung eines Finanzausgleichs für die Europäische Union. 2000.

Band 98 Marion Hübner: Ökodumping? Umweltpolitik in internationalen Oligopolmärkten. 2000.

Band 99 Christhart Bork: Steuern, Transfers und private Haushalte. Eine mikroanalytische Simulationsstudie der Aufkommens- und Verteilungswirkungen. 2000.

Band 100 Norbert Eichler: Die Probleme des Gemeindefinanzausgleichs im Kooperativen Föderalismus. Eine ökonomische Analyse am Beispiel des Bundeslandes Nordrhein-Westfalen. 2000.

Band 101 Wolfgang Scherf: Der Länderfinanzausgleich in Deutschland. Ungelöste Probleme und Ansatzpunkte einer Reform. 2000.

Band 102 Stefan Dietrich Josten: Staatsverschuldung, intertemporale Allokation und Wirtschaftswachstum. Eine theoretische Analyse staatlicher Verschuldungspolitik in Modellen exogenen und endogenen Wachstums. 2000.

Band 103 Axel Breitbach: Steuerhinterziehung und Schattenwirtschaft aus gesamtwirtschaftlicher Sicht. 2000.

Band 104 Alexander Spermann: Negative Einkommensteuer, Lohnsubventionen und Langzeitarbeitslosigkeit. 2001.

Band 105 Michael Broer: Der kommunale Finanzausgleich in Hessen. Historische Darstellung und ökonomische Analyse unter besonderer Berücksichtigung der Schlüsselzuweisungen. 2001.

Band 106 Jan-Paul Ritscher: Der Einsatz von Finanzderivaten unter einer modernisierten Schuldenstrukturpolitik des Bundes. 2002.

Band 107 Martin Gasche: Dynamische Fiskalpolitik. Makroökonomische Wirkungen der Fiskalpolitik in einem Real Business Cycle-Modell. 2003.

Band 108 Felix Brosius: Internationaler Steuerwettbewerb und Koordination der Steuersysteme. 2003.

Band 109 Claudia Hensberg: Eigennützige Regierungen im fiskalischen Wettbewerb um Kapital. 2003.

Band 110 Hans-Martin Grambeck: Konsumsteuerreformen und Konsumbesteuerung. Eine vergleichende Analyse und Bewertung verschiedener Konsumsteuermodelle unter besonderer Berücksichtigung der Probleme in offenen Volkswirtschaften. 2003.

Band 111 Antje Draheim: Probleme der finanzpolitischen Willensbildung in Europa. Eine kritische Analyse der europäischen Haushalts- und Finanzverfassung. 2004.

Band 112 Robert Nuscheler: On Competition and Regulation in Health Care Systems. 2005.

Band 113 Guido K. Raddatz: Das Eigenmittelsystem der Europäischen Union. 2005.

Band 114 Markus Euler: Ansatzpunkte für eine Reform des Finanzierungssystems der Europäischen Union. 2005.

Band 115 Marco Penske: Finanzierung der Gesetzlichen Krankenversicherung – Probleme und Reformoptionen. 2006.

Band 116 Pascal Krimmer: Demographie, Erwerbsbeteiligung, Steuerreformen und Steueraufkommen. Langfristige Auswirkungen von Steuerreformen. 2008.

Band 117 Frank Blasch: Steuerreformen und Unternehmensentscheidungen. Eine empirische Analyse der deutschen Steuerpolitik mit besonderem Schwerpunkt auf die Steuerreform 2000. 2008.

Band 118 Tobias Arens: Inter- und intragenerative Umverteilung im deutschen Steuer-Transfer-System. Langfristige Wirkungen im Lebenszyklus. 2009.

Band 119 Áron Kiss: Essays in Political Economy and International Public Finance. 2009.

Band 120 Tanja Kirn: Anreizwirkungen von Finanzausgleichssystemen. 2010.

Band 121 Sonja Kastin: Die Finanzierung von Agglomerationen über die Finanzausgleichssysteme in der Bundesrepublik Deutschland. Eine theoretische und empirische Bestandsaufnahme. 2011.

Band 122 Margarita M. Kalamova: Essays in International Trade and Public Economics. 2012.

www.peterlang.de

Peter Lang · Internationaler Verlag der Wissenschaften

Olaf Münster

Economic Integration and National Economic Policy

Frankfurt am Main, Berlin, Bern, Bruxelles, New York, Oxford, Wien, 2011.
XII, 182 pp., num. tab. and graph.
ISBN 978-3-631-61817-2 · hb. € 44,80*

The ongoing European integration together with global economic integration has caused apprehension in the public that national governments are losing their independence in economic policy. Especially, increased capital mobility is assumed to restrain the tax setting behavior of a national government – in the end constraining the scope and shape of government spending on public infrastructure, social services and other matters. By examining specific fiscal topics related to the current debate on economic integration, this book highlights aspects of the broader framework of fiscal competition. It develops further insight into the interaction of economic integration and public policy showing the scope and limits of national fiscal policy in an era of ongoing economic integration.

Content: Does Economic Integration Eliminate a Government's Ability to Independently Redistribute Income? · Regional Infrastructure and Tax Competition with Two Instruments · Economic Integration and the Taxation of Multinationals · Capital Tax Competition in the Light of Agglomerations Economies